Norse Mythology

Learn About Viking History, Myths and Legends

(A Comprehensive and Fascinating Guide Into Viking Life)

Rodrigo Butler

Published By **Bella Frost**

Rodrigo Butler

All Rights Reserved

Norse Mythology: Learn About Viking History, Myths and Legends (A Comprehensive and Fascinating Guide Into Viking Life)

ISBN 978-1-77485-550-8

No part of this guidebook shall be reproduced in any form without permission in writing from the publisher except in the case of brief quotations embodied in critical articles or reviews.

Legal & Disclaimer

The information contained in this ebook is not designed to replace or take the place of any form of medicine or professional medical advice. The information in this ebook has been provided for educational & entertainment purposes only.

The information contained in this book has been compiled from sources deemed reliable, and it is accurate to the best of the Author's knowledge; however, the Author cannot guarantee its accuracy and validity and cannot be held liable for any errors or omissions. Changes are periodically made to this book. You must consult your doctor or get professional medical advice before using any of the suggested remedies, techniques, or information in this book.

Upon using the information contained in this book, you agree to hold harmless the Author from and against any damages, costs, and expenses, including any legal fees potentially resulting from the application of any of the information provided by this guide. This disclaimer applies to any damages or injury caused by the use and application, whether directly or indirectly, of any advice or information presented, whether for breach of contract, tort, negligence, personal injury, criminal intent, or under any other cause of action.

You agree to accept all risks of using the information presented inside this book. You need to consult a professional medical practitioner in order to ensure you are both able and healthy enough to participate in this program.

Table of contents

Introduction 1

Chapter 1: A Review Of Norse Peoples And Cultures 3

Chapter 2: Asgard As Well Valhalla The Seat Of Divine Divinity.. 16

Chapter 3: Patron God: Odin............................. 23

Chapter 4: God Of War: Thor 28

Chapter 5: Trickster God: Loki........................... 35

Chapter 6: Minor Gods Balder, Freyr, And Freya 41

Chapter 7: Yggdrasil: The Tree In The Middle Of The Seven Realms 50

Chapter 8: The Golden Apples And Other Tales Of Divine Mortality.. 56

Chapter 9: Tales Of The Giants: Jotunheim 62

Chapter 10: The Mead Of Suttungr: Poetic Inspiration 68

Chapter 11: Ragnarok: The Nordic Myth It's Not The Movie.. 75

Chapter 12: Trolls: Rock-Dwelling Outsiders 85

Chapter 13: Valkyries: Friendly Spirits Or Fiendish Sprites?.. 90

Chapter 14: Elves And Dwarves: Creatures Of The Sky And Earth 97

Chapter 15: Midgard And The Humans 104

Chapter 16: Beowulf The Dark Twilight Of Norse Mythology And Early Christianity 111

Chapter 17: Additional Enchanting Stories And Figures.. 119

Chapter 18: The Aesir Gods As Well As Goddesses 124

Chapter 19: Vanir Gods And Goddesses 158

Chapter 20: Creation Of The Cosmos 165

Chapter 21: What We Can Utilize Viking Information Today 179

Conclusion 183

Introduction

In all likelihood, the Vikings have a prominent place in the imagination of many. In everything from Marvel's Thor as well as its subsequent sequels, to How to Train Your Dragon and its sequels. Popular culture has made fun from Norse mythology. The actual history and mythology as it turns out is likely to be just as intriguing as the screen adaptations. It is believed that the Norse are a collection of tribes that were bound by common linguistics and mythological traditions that were spread across a vast geographical region. The information we have about this society today comes mostly from the expeditions as well as the raids and settlements that were the work of Vikings.

The themes that are the basis of Viking and Nordic legends, generally they are reminiscent of the themes of many other mythologies. Magic can be a great way to explain the mysterious heroes and have strength and wisdom to spare. Gods are a bit tricky and must be approached with caution. difficult journeys are taken as battles are fought, and warriors are made. The constant reminder of the fragility of our lives and the uncertainty of the harvest and land, destiny and fate. Trust, courage and sacrifice are inexpensible to an enormous amount of wit and wisdom. the tricks needed to deceive God or trick an enemy, as well as the ability to figure out the best way to secure the land and its power. In addition, there is the constant desire for adventure and the desire to reach the ultimate glory.

From the Nordic pantheon of gods to the legendary exploits of Vikings, Norse mythology offers an array of thrilling adventure as well as magical adventures and romantic stories. Thus, take on these tales keeping an old Viking quote in your mind: "A tale is but half told when a single person is the one to tell the story." Here are the tales shared by the diverse peoples of this vibrant and rich culture.

Chapter 1: A Review Of Norse Peoples And Cultures

The Scandinavian sea-faring population of Norway, Denmark, and Sweden--were great explorers and astonished world travellers. Also, this loose group of peoples also established themselves to Finland, Greenland, and Iceland. These six countries form the foundation of what we today consider as Nordic culture. They left their mark on history during the first half of the modern age, beginning around the 8th century and ending in the 11th century CE. This is the time when their travels and military activities--threw them far away from their homeland and into the public imagination. The majority of the time, we refer to this diverse population by the name of "Vikings," but in truth, the term originally "Viking" was a verb. That is it was people from the Nordic people were for a long time an assortment of diverse tribes who had settled into agricultural communities across Scandinavia and other regions, however because of a myriad of external influences the peoples of these tribes resorted the form of Vikings, raiding and plundering other communities. In some instances, the Vikings established themselves in these other countries, and spread their mythology and culture across Europe.

The Nordic peoples, just like the Celts weren't an unified collective of individuals. The Vikings were a collective of different tribes with similarities in their languages, culture texts and traditions, as well as different styles of art. They were not a distinct group led by a single leader, or a single nation. They were scattered and settled in many locations, as mentioned in the previous paragraph. However, this diverse group of people made an enormous influence on Europe during in the Middle Ages, with their attacks and ultimately settlements that helped spread their influence across Europe and even beyond.

The reason they left their initial settlements is a subject for discussion, although most historians believe that a variety of factors were involved. There was a first issue with the issue of population pressure. There wasn't enough arable land for the population growth of the North. Therefore, the Vikings made raids to augment the resources they had in their possession, and to establish roots in specific regions. The harsh northern climate could also be a reason because growing crops and keeping afloat was not an easy task. When there were poor harvests and poor harvests, the Vikings were basically forced to leave the area.

It was also a matter of Vikings relations with Europe. In the first place the Vikings weren't Christians at this time and, therefore, they did not have a problem with robbing and pillaging foreigners in their customs and practices that were foreign to them. It's always easier to strike at people who are culturally and religiously different to you. Additionally there was a growing trade imbalance. When most of Europe was Christianized the regions began to oppose trade with pagans for example, the Vikings. So, what had previously were peaceful transactions turned into violent invasions. Vikings were required to engage in military force to survive. Additionally Many of the victims of the Viking raids were easily snatched up. The Christians were not allowed to fight in the church or on holy grounds; in the case of Vikings they had no such limit. The majority of communities which were targeted by Viking raids were unable to fight an argument.

In the end it was the time that the Nordic peoples were a-Viking as they were enticed by the promise of fame and adventure. This Norse belief that warriors who died were accepted in Valhalla by Odin definitely energised a robust warrior culture to set into unknown lands to engage in new combats. As eldest sons were the ones to inherit all the wealth and land of their fathers and their families, there was plenty of second sons that could only get these riches by going to battle or going on war. Furthermore, conflicts over power within Nordic areas were not unusual. Certain Vikings would prefer to go to try their luck elsewhere rather than serve under a king who was unpopular. For instance when Harald Fairhair was able to bring Norway under his rule and control, a number of minor chieftains from the region thought it was better to move elsewhere and leave rather instead of submitting to his rule.

The Vikings were able to launch these kinds of raids and be successful at it depended on several aspects. In the first place, they were skilled ship-builders, whose massive and massive battleships were robust enough to withstand the turbulent oceans that surrounded the European coastline. In actual fact they were the only ones to have Vikings reached all up to America in the millennium prior to when Columbus embarked on the"New World. "New World". Viking ships were different in the sense that they utilized an overlapping plank for their hulls--also known as lapstrake. This gave them a few advantages. First, this type of building ships resulted in extremely flexible vessels that could stand up to extreme storms without breaking or leaks. They were also quicker, more light and sleeker than other kinds of ships in the time of this. Thirdly, these larger narrower, more narrow ships with thinner bottoms could reach farther inland than the normal European ship. They could travel an additional 100 or so miles to attack or build a fortified base. This added extra maneuverability, as well as the possibility of surprise.

Vikings were incredibly proud of their vessels, and they continue to be an emblem of Norse culture until today. For the Vikings the ships were a symbol of strength and could carry their passengers across oceans in massive battles and in the afterlife. A lot of Vikings were buried on their vessels, or placed on a tiny boat which symbolized their status as warriors. Additionally, the vessel symbolized sustenance. In times of crisis the ship would provide food and hope to people. The distinctive appearance of Viking ships is recognizable today, as an indicator for Viking history as would any book or tale that is left by the author.

Alongside their stunning vessels in addition, the Vikings were formidable warriors, as well as, before that, they were skilled traders. The entire society embraced this "warrior" idea. A mature male was always armed while moving around and even at home. A sword is always at hand in close proximity, in the night. The honor-based society demanded that men protect their honour, their families and their homes at all times. Like the knight's tradition it was commonplace to settle disputes. The majority of men were not financially affluent enough to have swords which were among the most costly weapons to manufacture, however every man had an chainmail or leather padding. The most well-known weapons was spears since it contained the lowest amount of iron, which was the most valuable element in weaponry in the time.

Although the Vikings were the first to have written alphabets, the social stories and traditions were mostly passed on through oral transmission. Without vellum or paper it was difficult to keep documents written down. So, much of what we know about Viking culture was recorded more than the actual occasions and customs themselves. In many cases, these writings were written by Christianized groups, and consequently they have a certain bias in the texts. The subject will be addressed later in the book at various points.

The Vikings had a loosely-organized system of governmentthat was known as the "Thing". The Thing was basically an adult male gathering in the community to make decisions about the laws, settle disputes and decide local justice. Instead of tribunals that were improvised and ad hoc tribunals, the Thing was a imposed system that had regular meetings and highly skilled leaders who studied the essential codes that the society was required to live. Thus even in a world which did not have a long-standing tradition of written law it was clear that the Vikings were bound by certain cultural norms and legal frameworks that were codified and uniform. These gatherings were also the basis for other activities of the culture: marriages were planned, feasts were held and alliances were made. It is possible to imagine how much was consumed in mead and ale and also.

These times were also an opportunity to share stories and to spread gossip and news within the community. This is how Norse mythology and its associated pagan beliefs were spread through these early societies. The core of the universe is Yggdrasil The Tree of Life, out of which grew the Nine Worlds, home to gods and goddesses, humans and all that is. The gods and goddesses reside in Asgard in Valhalla and humankind is in Midgard. (Some of this might be familiar to readers of Thor: the Marvel Universe version of Thor.) It is true that the Giants also have an entire world, as do the dwarves and elves, with fire and ice. Then there's Hel, the Underworld. The complex world of mythology and religion is complex and fascinating like every other great civilization's tale about itself.

We should not forget that the Norse were originally traders and farmers. After a time, due to the pressures that were beyond their control, they were made Vikings. The religious beliefs they adhered to as well as the legends they constructed existed prior to the Viking time period. Vikings were the messengers dispersing this culture across Europe and further. The slow decline of Viking culture began with spreading of Christianity and, at the time of the 12th century the Nordic countries had been largely Christianized. It didn't necessarily mean that the old stories were lostor the traditional ways of life were discarded in the first place. In fact, we retain them to this day.

Goddesses and Gods

Pantheons of Norse gods and goddesses is diverse similar to how the Nordic people were. There are some well-known figures that are seen across time and space which suggests a shared mythological beliefs. Additionally, the long-lasting popularity of mythologies as well as legends is undisputed, considering the ubiquity of Thor at the modern box office.

The gods that appear with regularity are often skilled and brave warriors such as Odin and Thor which you'll be able to read about further below. Nordic mythology favors the powerful, particularly during the times of the Vikings who were excellent warriors of their own. One of the characteristics of gods and goddesses in all mythology is that they're highly adaptable, although Thor is the exception to this. In contrast to the Greco-Roman pantheons of gods The Nordic gods are derived from various sources, including Denmark, Norway, Sweden, and beyond. As such, the behavior and traits of gods and goddesses may differ in accordance with the material from which they originate. Additionally, the myths which introduce us to the gods and goddesses shift as time passes to accommodate the different needs of society in different times. This is the case for all mythological stories.

The myths that surround mythological gods and goddesses from Norse mythology, as is the case with the mythologies of all kinds--are generally stories that seek to establish a common culture or serve as a warning. The reason for this is that myths are used in order to help us remember the person we are and where we came from, and also to protect the good qualities of a specific style of living. However myths can be presented as parables, warning us against the risks of challenging a particular culture or value. When we hear these stories in the present it is possible that we do not believe in how to judge the "goodness" of this lifestyle, as our values are likely to be different. However, they provide insight into what heroics and triumph or villainy or trial meant to certain group of people in a specific moment in time. In this way, they are fascinating to read about and take lessons from, providing us with a glimpse into a past society that is so different from our current.

Gods and Goddesses in these myths are also designed to either represent an ideal for humans to strive toward--a kind of role model, or to deter certain types of behaviour. But, as Gods or Goddesses, they may be unpredictable and unpredictable, and not always reliable or not always a threat. They are still figures of awe and reverence due to their supernatural abilities and gifts in spite of what they do and the power they seem to have over humankind makes us want to go back time and time again to the fascinating stories.

Chapter 2: Asgard As Well Valhalla The Seat Of Divine Divinity

The first of all of the Nine Worlds, Asgard is the place where gods and goddesses dwell as well as Valhalla is the mysterious Hall of the Fallen. The Tree of Life, Yggdrasil and the Nine Worlds develop as do its activities in the chaos of the human race (Midgard), Asgard reigns in the top position. One of the most important aspects of Nordic mythology lies the belief that there exists some kind of the afterlife. However, it's complex due to competing theories of what it might mean. Asgard is where warriors strive to reach the top.

The word Asgard refers to "Enclosure to the Aesir," the Aesir being one of the branches of the pantheon, which is the most famous branch, that comprises Odin along with Thor, Loki and Freya among other. The word comes from the ancient Germanic distinction between utangard and Innangard. It is essentially that what is inside the fence, or innangard is civilized and orderly, and that which exists outside, called utangard, is wild and unruly. So, right from the foundational concepts of Nordic mythology there is a distinct distinction between us and Other Innangard: We belong to Asgard or Midgard - inside the fence, regulated and civilized. You are not. Anyone who is who are not inside the fence will be thought to be wild, foreign and uncivilized. This is a common theme across every culture throughout history, as we discover how to define ourselves not so much by what we're not, and not by who we are. The rules of Asgard are, therefore, to be the foundational principles of those who adhere to this belief system. In direct opposition with Asgard is Jotunheim which is the home of the giants, which we'll find out the details in chapter 9.

The gods of Asgard are a central part of Nordic mythology in a variety of ways. They play a role in the protection of humans in the face of the forces that cause chaos (often depicted as giants). They are also rulers and as such, require respect and obedience from humans. Thirdly, while gods are higher than humans, they are dependent on fate, or wyrd, a concept that lies at foundation of the Viking lifestyle. So, there is no "supreme being" like we find within Christianity or Islam Instead gods are supernatural beings who have greater power than human beings, and the various gods had distinct responsibilities towards Midgard. They helped with the harvest and some assisted during battle. Still, other gods tended to families. While Odin was considered to be the godfather but he was also dependent on fate, and his vast knowledge was acquired only through hard efforts, not through divine rights. These gods and goddesses from Nordic mythology seem human in various ways.

In fact, the connection that exists between Asgard as well as Midgard is the main source of basis for the majority of Norse mythology. Interactions between gods from Asgard along with their humans counterparts Midgard comprise the majority of the action and are the moral axis of the mythological worldview.

This is not a stretch, surely since It was actually the Nordic people themselves who invented these mythological stories. As for the gods and goddesses, Asgard were extremely anthropomorphic gods, and their interactions between them and humans were vital. For instance, the legend that gods were have mated with humans to form royal families was a central principal for Nordic society. Also, there was a culture of reciprocity. If humans performed rituals in a right way, they would be able to expect offerings from gods. The gods are rewarded with praise and reverence, and humans gain excellent crops or victories in combat. This is a typical motif, naturally, in many religions and mythologies. In Nordic myths Asgard as well as Midgard are joined by something more symbolic than the Rainbow Bridge, which is a promise from the sky.

Valhalla The Valhalla Hall, also known as known as the Hall of the Fallen, is a fascinating alternative to the afterlife. It's definitely an ideal place for those who fight, since those who reside in Valhalla are engaged in combat or play throughout the day, proving their worth through continuous bravery and strength. When evening comes around healing is complete and the feasting starts. They have an endless quantity of meat coming from the magical boar Saehrimnir which is revived following each meal, only to be slaughtered to make another dinner. Their mead is magical, and originates out of the cow's udder Heidrun and whose milk is never stopped flowing. This is why Valhalla is the continuation of the glorious Viking life with an added bonus of immortality, at least for a while. Odin gathers fallen warriors to fill Valhalla to prepare for the final battle, Ragnarok. the world is bound to be destroyed. All good things have to be ended it is believed.

The process of gaining entry to Valhalla is a relatively easy process: Warriors who die during fight gain entry into Valhalla and those who die from illness or old age are buried in hell--Hel. This is sure to encourage the Vikings to pillage, raid and fight without doubt. There are a few accounts that state famous warriors don't in reality end up in Valhalla The premise is that the choice rests on Odin. It's his hall at the very least and he fills the hall with the people he likes the most.

Even though Asgard as well as Valhalla have received the greatest acceptance in our current knowledge of Viking cosmology However, there are other destinations to go to after death for Nordic peoples. There's Hel Of course and it is not to get confused with the Christian notion about Hell; Hel is merely an alternative realm, the underworld, in which the deceased generally live their lives exactly as they lived their lives. Freya is said to invite people into her hall, called Folkvang, the place where people gather. Also, those who die at sea could end up living with the giantess Ran. The notions of divine reincarnation and immortality in Nordic mythology stem from the concept that there are Nine Realms: We all live in one of them at some point or another and until the time of death.

Chapter 3: Patron God: Odin

A surprisingly confusing characters in mythology, Odin is both a poet and a warrior who seeks wisdom as well as a tricker, a patron to the rulers and outlaws. Odin spends just as many hours in the world of Asgard as well as Valhalla as he spends within its boundaries, and frequently goes on lengthy and arduous explorations of knowledge for its own purpose. The god of the gods is the chief, Odin is alternately called "Allfather" and "The Master of Fury." The very name implies that he's the breath of life. without him, there'd be no pantheon or Asgard and certainly no Midgard. However, despite all this, Odin could be an extremely conflicted and conflicted persona and.

Odin was, naturally extremely closely linked to war, just as the Viking culture was, but how he was seen by the first Vikings is different from the way that contemporary perceptions of him have been constructed. Indeed, the earlier versions of Odin's tales indicate that he was not just a warrior chieftain however, he was a vicious inciter of war, that is, he would entice otherwise peaceful people into fighting war. This was his way to, as it was observed, to identify the most skilled soldiers on the battlefield to gather his own army at Valhalla to fight the death all world. He did not seem to be concerned about what the reason for fighting or who was victorious the battle, but instead, revealed his character in the process of war itself.

He was a favored player It is a fact and he allied his only with the elite warriors and their families. In reality the royal families that originate from Nordic tribes were believed to be a part of Odin's lineage. He also joined with the berserkers, notoriously fierce (some might say crazy) Germanic warriors who took no prisoners. Evidently, Odin liked the berserkers not only due to their fierce combat skills, but also due to their connection to animals and the name itself translates to "bear-shirts." Odin himself was represented by ravens as well as the wolves. The animal spirits help inspire a warrior with the intensity of a bear or wild wolf, which is a terrifying experience for any opponent, surely--and also to recognize the connection between all living creatures and not just humans.

In contrast to Odin's adulation of the noble and powerful fighters from the Norse as well as Germanic tribes He was also the god patron of the outlaws. Odin was a ally to the outlaws with intelligence who acted against the rules of society. He was impressed by their determined and fervent dedication to their own rules. There is a legend that claims Odin himself was removed from Asgard for a long time because other gods and goddesses would not like to be identified with him, as poor was his image among the human race turned out to be.

Alongside his warrior traits, Odin is also linked to wisdom and poetry. He isn't just a symbol for the sexual Viking characteristics that immediately spring to your mind, but also embodies a feminine side in his search for beauty and understanding. Since the Nordic gods weren't all-powerful or omniscient - they needed to exert effort to attain their power-- Odin is always seeking wisdom. In reality, he's depicted as a god with only one eye with a depleted eye-socket due to the fact that he sacrificed an eye to acquire wisdom. There is also a well-known legend in which Odin suspended himself off his Tree of Life, Yggdrasil for nine nights and days without food or drink to discover the runes of magic. The last thing he boasted about at the conclusion of the experience was that the man "was fertilized and learned." The ordeal is a symbolic symbol of death and rebirth process, through which a sorcerer or shaman grows more powerful. Consider Gandalf as portrayed in Lord of the Rings returning as Gandalf the White after a fight with Balrog. Balrog.

Odin also spent a lot of his time wanderingaround, taking journeys to the Other Nine Worlds in order to gain more insight and, in turn more power. Some of these travels are more like lengthy contemplation; it is claimed that he traveled to far places while appearing asleep or dead. A different story in the book, "Baldur's Dreams," tells of Odin riding his eight-legged horse into the underworld to talk to an old priestess regarding his son. He once challenged the smartest of giants to a game of wits. The winner was awarded the head of the loser. Odin confronted the giant with a trick question which only Odin himself would be able to answer and then came back to Asgard with the prize.

Odin has also been associated with poetry and a person is only permitted to write poetry when Odin considers them worthy. Indeed, he snatched the poetry mead from the giants, and has only used it infrequently since.

Odin is, of course, is also the master of the dead, particularly of the dead warriors. The hall he calls Valhalla has such spirits Odin along with his Valkyrie aids bring the deceased to Asgard's most revered spot. Viking armies would often sacrifice their foes in the name of Odin to take prisoners, since it was expensive and heavy for an army of raiders aboard a boat.

Odin's fame as an Allfather is certainly evident from the many many roles he is required to play. The Norse considered Gods and Goddesses in their religion as guardians of all living and dead things. In actual they were the guardians in their own Nine Worlds and held the whole of the universe together. Odin himself was the chief of this noble, but turbulent project. His sagacity and understanding was crucial to preserving the authority bestowed by Yggdrasil.

Chapter 4: God Of War: Thor

Thor the god of thunder, the powerful god who thunders and is Odin's child is the best depiction for the heroic warrior. His strength is as unparalleled as is his honor, and he spends his days defending Asgard from encroaching enemies--particularly the giants. He is a wonderful human companion to the people who reside in Midgard. He is far more of a modern god than Odin. He performs his duties with unwavering dedication which is what makes him the most adored God in the Norse canon to this day, in not the least part because of Chris Hemsworth and Marvel Comics.

As the ultimate god of war, Thor certainly looks the part. As opposed to the slimy Odin with his squinty eye Thor has a muscular physique and is strong, and he is adorned with the belt of strength that grants him unrivalled physical strength. Also the Hammer, Mjollnir, that he can almost never be without. For the Norse thunder was a symbol of Thor himself, and lightning represented the hammer striking him against giants or other foes from the Nine Worlds. Thor was depicted as flying through the skies in a chariot driven by goats (an important domestic animal of people of the Nordic tribal groups).

A lot of the stories about Thor are about his battles against the main enemy of Asgard, the Jotunheimr's giants. The giants symbolize destruction and chaos; they are barbaric, utangard, and outside the boundaries. They escape with Thor's hammer and hold it until Thor is able to produce the sister of his, Freya in marriage. However, Thor disguises himself as Freya and then presents his self to giants of their hall of great size. As they put his hammer in front of him, as was the custom at weddings--he picked the hammer, shedding his disguise and struck every giant within the space dead. Thor will not surrender his hammer easily since it is his primary weapon in battle to defend and maintain the order and civilized character that is Asgard as well as Midgard.

One of his main adversaries is Jormungand The massive sea serpent that is encircling Midgard and is threatening to devour Midgard completely. They battle in the past, but they finally end their battle in the final fight of Ragnarok (more details to be revealed in chapter 11). In one tale, Thor accepts shelter from the giant in order to fish at sea. Thor kills an animal to fish with its head. He was searching for a huge prey, in fact. After catching an ocean serpent he's carried overboard and dragged down into the depths of the ocean. The seafloor is able to stabilize him enough to pull the reel, and draw the beast into. Just as he was planning to take out the beast by hammering it The giant cut through the line, fearful for his life. But, they are fated to be reunited.

Apart from hunting enemies to eliminate the enemy, one of Thor's most important tasks in Midgard included blessing people and their actions. Runic inscriptions discovered in Nordic ruin sites call for Thor to bless individuals, the land as well as the words. Thor was invoked during wedding ceremonies to bless the union and bless the land on the which their home would be constructed. The hammer he smashed into the ground actually served two purposes: to smash enemies as well as bless the people he loved. In fact, as legends tell us, Thor routinely slaughtered his goats (the ones that drove his car over the heavens) then ate them and after which he gathered the bones together. The hammer's strike on the bones Hammer, they come back to life, allowing them to begin the journey and over.

Due to this power to bless people and the earth, Thor is also a god of fertility and agriculture. He is a god of the sky for sure as lightning and thunder are definitely connected to the most powerful rain that gives life to crops. He is the one who controls the weather and, consequently the quality in the yield. His wife, who is seldom mentioned, wears beautiful golden locks. It's certainly a symbol reference to the fields of grain. Thor the god of the sky is allied with Sif who is the Earth goddess, who fills the earth with grains along with food and drink for everyone the people of Midgard.

Thor was even more well-known in the time of the Vikings. The reasons are both apparent and obscure. It is obvious that Thor was the ideal physical and mental image of the warrior-hero. Honorable, brave, and strong-- what everyone Viking wanted to be. Not as obvious is that he was also the god of the second-tier of society. He was not a representative of the elite, leaders or the nobility; more, Thor was the patron of the military, generals as well as the soldiers. Odin was a god of safeguarding those in the top classes while Thor is the god of those who battle and risk their lives to protect the ruling class. Many myths show the antagonistic aspect of the relation between Odin as well as Thor. The myth that Odin removed Thor from Asgard is rooted in some myths however, it is primarily was a creation of the Marvel collection of films.

Another major reason Thor was popular in the period that of Vikings is the threat that was growing to Christianity. When Christianity first arrived in Europe it was a time when the Norse people were not worried. Other (pagan) religions have been extinct, as well as the Norse were able to adhere their own religion. However, during the period of the Vikings it was evident that Christianity wasn't like the other religions and was not a system that allowed the continuation of the ancient Nordic lifestyles and belief. Therefore, who would be better to safeguard those Vikings and their people than Thor who has always stood by them during moments of turmoil? One of the smallest acts of rebellion the Vikings used after the change of a number of Scandinavian rulers was to wear the Thor hammer Thor around their necks instead of the Christian cross. In good or bad ways the time of the Vikings ended in defeat, just like the gods of Ragnarok. the only thing we have left are the myths and legends which made them influential in past times.

Chapter 5: Trickster God: Loki

Dangerous and attractive, Loki is a wily and occasionally grumpy god with whom to negotiate. The fact that he is a mutable character in real world mythology makes his character in modern films look remarkably solid and heroic. In reality, when it comes to the stories about Loki He has very little, if none, redeeming traits. He longs to see the end of Asgard and, while sometimes he is playful but he is mostly violent. One could claim Loki is the most interesting god. Loki can be the most fascinating of the Nordic gods due to the fact that he is probably the most human. Self-serving and fragile, sometimes unruly and sometimes harsh, Loki speaks truth to the gods in a way heroes cannot.

In one of his last sly actions, Loki forces his way into the hall of Aegir which is among the greats and also the god of the Sea whom is hosting an celebration for all gods and goddesses. Loki obviously is not welcomed--in fact the mythology in itself doesn't make it crystal evident that Loki wasactually a god, but Loki is able to impress himself by invoking these rules. After being served a drink, Loki starts to tell scathing tales about the gods and goddesses who are present. He recounts their transgressions as well as their instances of cowardice, as well as instances when he had embarrassed them by his tricks. If they attempt to insult him He simply dismisses them and then returns an even worse insult at them. Thor who was not been present at this incident, returned to the hall and Loki immediately brought up how he was completely manipulated with the giant's representation Loki. Thor confronted Loki with his hammer and Loki retreats and cowers. But Loki has the final word, reminding all of the Gods and Goddesses of the world that time is through: Ragnarok is approaching, and he'll be content to see the world be destroyed.

On one side, it is unpalatable however, Loki is portrayed as a cruel and selfish person. However, when you read a counter-reading,

Loki is the only one of the deities who is open to addressing the truth. They are not perfect gods and goddesses and Loki is well aware of that. In spite of their strength as well as power, they may be weak and foolish. Loki seems to be the only one who can be said to be the one who can rise to the challenge of telling the truth.

Loki's origins are in contrast to his murky nature, too. In certain stories, he's an heir to a brutal giant and a mother with an unknown origin. She is described as an ethereal god or a giantess. In other stories, she is an unidentified species. In other words, he is a creature from a realm that is a mystery. And what could be more dangerous than a mysterious persona of power? Loki himself is frequently identified as one of the godfathers Hel, the kind leader of the underworld, of Jormungand the sea serpent which encircles Midgard and Thor's most formidable adversary and Fenrir the wolf, who is ultimately the final death of Odin. Loki's role within the mythology is highly doubtful and there aren't references to him that suggest Loki was ever worshipped the same way as the gods of the other gods were. He appears to serve as the symbol of disruption, a way to explain the reason why bad things appear to happen in a random manner.

His most famous part is the one that ended with the death of Balder Thor's brother, who was the beloved child of Odin. Balder was, according to all reports the most gorgeous and pure-hearted of gods. So, it seems obvious that Loki was extremely insecure about him as well as his stature. But, it was believed that Balder would pass away before his death. Therefore, Frigga, his mother was a traveler to every corner of the world to make everyone and everything swear not to harm her son. She made numerous promises, so that no one was concerned about the tiniest mistletoe that she didn't use to charm, thinking it was too small and insecure to harm her son. When Loki discovers this, he designs a mistletoe spear and, in typical Loki tricker style, places it into Hoder's hands. God,

Hoder. In the event that all gods have been invited to throw objects at Balder - this is good fun since everyone believes that he's invincible - Loki calls Hoder to drop the spear of mistletoe towards Baldur which kills him.

When Balder is taken back to hell, Gods ask Hel to take him back to the realm of the living as Balder is loved in all ways. Hel responds that he'd be more than content to see Balder to the world if all living things is mourning him, because it would show his unimaginable value. The word has been all over the world, and everyone mourns, with the exception of one giantess of frost called Tokk. Therefore, Hel requires that Balder remains within the realm of darkness. Naturally, it's later revealed that Tokk is in fact Loki disguised as Loki.

The issue is the issue of Loki is clearly a nefarious and scheming creature, that is susceptible to such jealousy that is so deadly dangerous. However there is a counter-reading that suggests Loki is a constant snitch to the realms of the gods and also the sharing of feelings with any person or thing. One can't help but think of Loki to be a depressing character, at least from a modern perspective (one that is influenced by modern-day psychology). In the eyes of Norse people who believed in the mythology, Loki was certainly a symbol for all the evil forces that were outside their control and couldn't be controlled through the logic of reason or by custom.

The gods of the other gods eventually have to punish Loki for his sinful actions by binding Loki to a rock inside the cave, where the poisonous snake drips upon him continually. Somehow his wife Sigyn is loyal to Loki and is devoted to collecting the poisonous drips using an empty bowl. Every now and then she has to get out of bed and take the bowl away and Loki is forced to writhe in pain while the poison drips down on him. In his agony, he writhed his movements caused seismic waves that rocked Midgard as well as the rest of Midgard. The man is held until the last battle of Ragnarok.

Although Loki is clearly a sinister persona, his place in the pantheon is a sign of the followers of this mythical religion. must be a method to explain the seemingly absurd evils that are sometimes committed to the world. Loki was a popular scapegoat. In our modern times, we see someone who is hated due to his inability to be a part of with the people who he wants to be accepted by. This is surely an indication of the end of the world.

Chapter 6: Minor Gods Balder, Freyr, And Freya

Even though Odin, Thor, and Loki are definitely most well-known among the Norse gods There were many gods equally significant in the Norse pantheon in the days that of the Vikings. Balder was well-known among Germanic people generally, and was considered the most beautiful, fairest and jovial of gods. Our information about him is in fragments, the most comprehensive of which pertains to his death. Freyr however, on contrary was among the gods that was most revered across the entire region. Since Freyr represented the God of agriculture and fertility It is easy to understand the reason. The twin of his, Freya, was the Norse goddess of love and was the female symbol of fertility.

The story of Balder's passing was outlined in the preceding chapter: Balder's jealousy caused Loki's death, and his final exile to Hel, the underworld. There are a few some fragments from other stories of Balder which contradict this harmless portrayal of the god who was martyred. Danish sources portray Balder as a man who is determined to be a part of war with a lot of bloodlust; in reality Balder appears to be like a warlord. Therefore, the most long-running Balder myth--that of his utterly passive acceptance of Loki's jealousy as well as his tragic fate -- may not accurately or even fully depict all the aspects of the way Balder's Norse god was seen during the period that of the Vikings. It's interesting that he's constantly praised as the god most loved by people If this is the case that he was loved by the Vikings is a valid logic that he would actually be a fierce and brave warrior. Most often, we create gods in our own image.

Freyr In contrast, Freyr is the god of health and abundance and health; to worship Freyr was to guarantee the harvest to be plentiful and an abundance of young children. He was often depicted as a god of abundance or as an animal counterpart, the Golden-Bristled Boar, an important source of food for the ancient Nordic as well as Germanic tribes. Images of him also show his virility--literally--by depicting him with a large phallus. He was the home of the elves as their king, even though this wasn't explicitly stated in the myths that survived. The elves are in general believed to be supernatural, but kind creatures, so Freyr's relationship with them definitely demonstrates this.

Freyr is also the owner of a stunning ship, which is likely to explain the Viking admiration for him. Ships were unquestionably essential to Viking warriors. Freyr's ship was able to have the ability to always receive an ideal breeze and could be amused to fold down so that it could be tucked away in the size of a carryall. This ship may also be a symbol of the ceremony of burying veteran sailors at sea and other similar ceremonies associated with small, robust vessels. It appears that Freyr's vessel fits into this particular ritualistic model.

The sister of his, Freya She is similar to that of the Roman goddess Venus in the symbol of sexual love and affection. In fact, Freya is portrayed as an unassuming goddess, who is seeking pleasures in the physical world and having expensive things. Loki even says that she had sexual relations with all Elves as well as the brother of her (though we all know that Loki does not necessarily exaggerate.). Freya is also in charge of the second dimension of hell named "Folkvang" as well as the warriors who were not selected by Odin to dwell in Valhalla typically resided in the underworld along with the god of love. It's not a bad way to conclusion, you could claim.

Freya also plays the role that of the volva. a type of sorcerer who traveled and would travel from town to city performing tiny acts of magic in exchange for food and lodging. This was common during Viking times in addition, Freya is their god of patronage. The role, which was once a source of great respect, started to lose its luster when Christian concepts spread throughout the North. However, Freya herself continued to be an inspiration and source of worship. the source of inspiration.

Also, it is believed by certain researchers to be the case that Freya along with Odin's wife Frigg is the exact same goddess. The attributes each goddess is assigned are similar enough to be nearly identical. Furthermore to that, the name Freya is essentially "lady"--that is her name is an inscription but not a real name. The German word"frau", which means "lady" originates from Freya.

While there is very little information available on the gods of the minor gods, they remain interesting and unique in their role within

Nordic mythology and culture. Baldur loved by everyone, was also a formidable warrior. Freyr and Freya provided fertile crops and abundant crops to the land, a crucial role that is difficult to quantify. There are numerous gods that are part of the pantheon each one having their own distinct role in the Nordic theology. Chapter 17 lists a few of them, together with their respective attributes. Also, in case we're not paying attention that, in Nordic mythology, gods and goddesses don't have to be the only supernatural beings. There are giants, elves, dwarfs Trolls, giants, and Valkyries all over the place. Find out more about all these intriguing characters.

Legends and Culture

Norse stories and myths weave together a tight web of myths and legends that provide information on how people behave and how they should behave and the reasons why the world functions in the way it does. This is the purpose of legends, myths and morality stories are designed to do telling the reader (or the modern-day the reader) the good behavior of people and how badly they are punished, and what morals we should hold to. They're our links to the beautiful Northern past, revealing about who the characters were as well as what beliefs they held. They also provide explanations explaining how weather functions for instance when it was before meteorology. It's not a coincidence that in every mythological tradition there is the unavoidable gods of thunder (Zeus, Lugh, Thor) as well as many gods of the harvest and fertility (Freyr and Freya). These myths speculate on why certain events happen, by granting powers to gods as well as other supernatural beings. This was a method to make sense of an unorganized world and understanding our role within it.

It also served as a means of protection In the event that you believe in a specific God or Goddess, or perform a certain ritual or follow the appropriate rituals, you will be able to avoid suffering and enjoy prosperity. It is also an opportunity to delegate to someone else the responsibility for things that are out that of the control of one's own ("It was too rainy this year to have a great crop" and "Our sacrifices to Freyr were not sufficient"). In addition, it is an excuse for celebration and feasting during the events are considered to be a sign of good luck.

Nordic cultures and their legends have many resemblances with mythological canons from other cultures The magic is everywhere and used to explain the mysterious characters have incredible strength, with divine roots and make the most of the hard-earned wisdom that they have acquired gods may be aids or tricksters in the right situation; there are plenty of adventures as well as romance that is complex and sometimes tragic; wars continue to be fought and warriors continue to be replaced. It is a constant reminder of the fragility of our lives and the uncertainty over the harvest and land cattle and children. The virtues of loyalty, bravery and sacrifice are the same virtues that stress collaboration for the common benefit are prevalent in the most storied texts. Since we are all interdependent, and without each other we wouldn't be able to coexist in any way.

Chapter 7: Yggdrasil: The Tree In The Middle Of The Seven Realms

From this massive and all-encompassing tree, beginnings of the universe is believed to be derived from Norse mythology. Yggdrasil is the root of all things, and out of it comes the Nine Worlds: The gods and goddesses, giants and Dwarves and elves, as well as men. The health of the entire universe is dependent on the health of this majestic tree. it only trembles once, at the very end, as Ragnarok closes in.

It's interesting that Norse mythology has trees to symbolize the centre all of creation. There is certainly a foundation in the actual environment where the Nordic people lived, which was lush and full of wild creatures. It is also noteworthy it is an organic living thing, not concrete plains or empty space. It also, is mortal, like the gods, just like humans are.

Yggdrasil is believed to be a friend to the sky, and is so high that it is difficult to be able to see its top peeking out over the clouds. Since its heights can be exhilarating, it is also capped by snow that melts and is deposited below giving life-giving dew as well as water to all the animals that are a part of its roots and branches. Its roots are untraceable since they go deep enough to plunge into the depths of the earth and are the only place that all living creatures can be found. The mysterious Tree of Life is not only a part of Nordic mythology, since it is mentioned in many sacred and mythological texts all over the world. The life-giving, long-living tree is surely a suitable symbol of the beginnings of the universe.

Yggdrasil is more than the tree standing by itself however, it is the focal point of activities and competitions, as well as other happenings. The gods have their daily meetings at the tree. It is a gathering place that has a spiritual significance. Odin naturally suspended himself in the trees for nine months to learn the secrets of the runes of the past. The tree as a gallows is a different symbol that has resonance across different religions. Odin is revived in the same time period, which is another evidence of the life-giving power of Yggdrasil. Certain, the tale of Odin's discovery of wisdom suggests that this tree holds the source of all knowledge significant. Bran Stark's Heart Tree (from The Game of Thrones series) definitely owes some respect to Nordic mythology.

There are creatures in the treethat perform different tasks. At the bottom there is a dragon, together with his serpent companions and a majestic eagle is found at the highest branches. The two rivals frequently exchange insults with the aid of Ratatoskr. A squirrel with a long, sharp teeth. One could imagine that the battles between the eagle and the dragon were a way to develop moral values that would determine which is more desirable, to stay near the ground or to fly high up in the air? Each animal would have their own opinion on this issue, and similar to many other aspects of Nordic thinking it is necessary to have a balance between both sides.

Although Asgard is always depicted in the sky, as most versions of heaven are, the origins of Yggdrasil are believed to be established in three different realms. Midgard which is the world of the men; Jotunheim which is the home of the giants, and Hel the underworld. This suggests that the success that the tree has is dependent on the coordination and collaboration between the three realms. If you look at it from an ancient perspective it is logical. Midgard could be the place that people from the Nordic people, also known as the Vikings took over our country. Jotunheim is a foreign land that were inhabited by people from other countries who's customs, behaviors and lifestyles were completely different from Vikings' home. Furthermore, Hel is the ultimate place that those who go from this world into the next. Valhalla along with Asgard are places of aspiration that only the most powerful warriors chosen by God will be. There has to be a different place for everyone else.

Actually, the layout of the Nine Worlds around the tree is a loose order of the significance of each world to what reason. Asgard is located high in the unobserved branches over the clouds, whereas Midgard is securely planted at the base of the tree and Hel is tucked away in the depths of the ground beneath its roots. The other realms -- of the giants, elves , the dwarves and other creatures -- are separated in a horizontal fashion from the trunk upwards the closest realms towards the trunk like Midgard could be a representation of the realm of innangard or what can be described as "inside the fence"--that that is well-known and recognizable. The regions further away of the trunk like Jotunheim could represent utangard or that it is "outside the fence"--that that is unexplored and alien, and is usually in danger.

It is also important to note that the farmsteads of all of the Nordic the world (and beyond, naturally) were built around a huge tree symbolizing Yggdrasil. This way, the farmstead itself can be thought of as an atom of the universe, and arranged in such an arrangement that acknowledges the significance of the Tree of Life. It is easy to see why Vikings are so determined to protect this lifestyle that is so deeply rooted is in their whole existence and their system of beliefs.

Chapter 8: The Golden Apples And Other Tales Of Divine Mortality

Norse mythology differs from other mythologies in the sense that the gods of Norse mythology are, obviously mortal. The Norse gods are very anthropomorphic--that is, they are portrayed most often as if they were simply larger-than-life humans. Odin can be described as a hyper-charged scholar looking for wisdom. Thor is the perfect warrior to whom the Vikings sought as a role model. They're also human-like creatures, even with greater power. Therefore, they have to consume a mysterious fruit, which is usually depicted as golden apples to fight off aging and the onset of death. Similar to most stories involving apples there are two aspects that are certain to be involved first, the fruit that the tale is told probably is not an actual apple (these were not known in Scandinavia in the period of Norse myth-making) Also, any kind of trouble is bound to follow.

Idun is a important, though less acknowledged goddess from Norse mythology. She is significant due to the fact that she is the one who keeps the Golden Apples or fruits of immortality. The gods have to eat one each day to keep their vitality and youth. It's evident clearly that these fruits are extremely valuable and would be the envy of any animal that didn't have them readily available.

It was discovered the fact that Odin, Loki, and another god were traveling on long travels in an extremely hostile region of the country. They were required to hunt oxen to feed their families However, when they attempted to cook the meat and found out that regardless of how long they hung the meat in the flame it would not cook. A voice over them finally called out: "I am the one stopping your food from cooking! I am in your land and I would like you to be sharing the food along with me." It was an eagle looking out over their camp. So , the gods agreed and the eagle flew down to collect his portion. But he took all the desirable parts and left the gods with less appealing components. This irritated Loki particularly. He grabbed a huge branch and began to slash at the eagle, using his improvised spear however, to his delight the eagle snatched the branch in its claws and flew to the sky, carrying Loki along with it. Loki begged the eagle for him to drop down but the eagle was unable until Loki offered to deliver Idun, the Goddess of Heaven. Idun and her magical fruit.

It turns out that the eagle was actually one of the gigantics Thjazi who could cover himself up as an Eagle. Loki was aware that he needed to fulfill his promise in the sense that Thjazi was an imposing giant with a fortress that was high within the mountain ranges, from where the giant could unleash his wrath over the fields down below. Then, Loki convinced Idun to follow him, claiming that he'd discovered extraordinary fruits that were superior to her golden apples. She continued to follow him until they came to the way to the fortress of the giant, when the eagle appeared and took her into his palace.

The gods and goddesses realised that Idun as well as her gold apples had gone, they were upset, to say the least. Their skin began to wrinkle and their hair began to turn grey; their strength began to diminish. Then, Loki was identified as the person who was the last to be seen by Idun and was forced to share the tale. (Actually it is possible to conclude it was because the effects of age were taking their effects on him, and so it wasn't for his own benefit--and that's Loki's main concern that we all know--to keep his story from being revealed to continue.)

Freya the goddess of love Freya, the goddess of love, gave Loki some of her feathers. It enabled him to transform into bird. Loki was able to fly to Thjazi's fortress, where--coincidentally--he found that the giant had gone out hunting, leaving Idun alone. Loki quickly changed her into a nut, for convenience of transport, it is believed--and returned to Asgard as quickly as possible.

The giant, however, was able to see him flying away and realized the fact that Idun was gone, so he repositioned his back on the eagle, and pursued Loki with all the force. The gods of other gods were also eagerly waiting for Loki's return, and believed that the giant would engage in a battle. They therefore constructed an edifice of kindling near the border to prevent the giant from entering Asgard. When Loki crossed the border The gods set the fire to the kindling and the giant/eagle crashed into it, breaking into flames.

While this story is that is of special interest to be found in Nordic mythology, it's not the only story that reveals the incredibly mortal aspect of Viking gods. The story of the Balder's death, which is recounted in Chapter 5--who was more than just loved by all but was as some stories suggest the mythology, a god of war. The story about Ragnarok (see Chapter 11) and it is related to the end of The Nine Worlds. It also reveals-perhaps most important--the ever-present notion of wyrd, also known as fate: We're all and humans alike--in an intricate web of destiny that cannot be predicted nor manage. This is completely logical from an Viking perspective: Their world was unpredictable of weather and harvests as well as of wars and territories The only thing that was known was the possibility of death. The mythologies of all people are crafted by analyzing their own personal experiences. This is the reason every mythology in the world contains stories of the afterlife or the underworld, the afterlife, and most of all stories about immortality because that is the only thing in all of our lives that we take for granted: death is inevitable. It's not that it's only negative or demoralizing. Rather it could also be an motivation to show yourself as an excellent warrior or build a magnificent home. The time to make the most of it is as it is available.

Chapter 9: Tales Of The Giants: Jotunheim

The significance of the giants in Nordic mythology is incomparable The giants aren't only the rulers of some or more of the Nine Worlds, but they are also the antithesis of gods. In the irony prevalent in many mythological stories they serve to demonstrate what we shouldn't as, and serve as a counterpoint to what gods and as a result, human beings should be similar to. They are essential to the stories because you can't have heroes and gods without creatures and "others." Mythology is the basis for the way a culture is defined and, in turn, we identify ourselves by what aren't. So, the giants have to exist to provide the sake of a moral compass within this cosmology. Just as The Avengers require Thanos to show off their talents, bravery and morality. It is impossible to know what is right if it is not possible to determine the wrong.

The name "giants" is actually misleading to begin with. It is merely the abbreviated form of the earlier Germanic phrase, called jotnar which is more precise to mean "devourers." This is why our concepts of giants, derived from tales such like Jack and the Beanstalk or in recent times, from the realm of Harry Potter are centered mostly on the massive and possibly threatening physical appearance of giants. In the context of Norse Cosmology, giants are considered to be threatening due to their symbolic association with disorder, chaos and the consuming of the well-organized and principled. The mythology of many myths is actually designed in this waythat the things we do not understand seem chaotic and unorganized We must defend our ordered and properly-organized way of living. The giants that are featured in Norse mythology actually pose the only threat to existence itself. They symbolize decay and entropy.

Furthermore to that, it is important to realize that, according to the first creation myth of Norse belief, a large portion of the gods are giants or part devourers. Odin himself is half-giant. Thor is 3 quarters descended from giants. Therefore, it is worth noting that the presence of the giant is vital for the entire system to function. That means that the purpose of gods isn't to take on or eliminate the giants, but rather they are there to keep their appetite in check and ensure that their chaos is kept at bay to ensure that the universe can maintain its controlled order. If darkness is not present, then there will be no understanding of light.

The giants are a recurring theme throughout the stories as disruptors to the order of things as we've seen in the tales described above: Thjazi's stealing from Idun along with the golden apple threaten the eternality that the gods have of Asgard and the loss of Thor's hammer could threaten his ability to safeguard the security of Midgard. Another fantastic tale of giant mischief is about one of the strongest of those giants Hrungnir who is also in a battle against Thor.

Odin--who is filled with mischief and chaos sometimes--decides to go to Odin, one of the greats from Jotunheim which is the name given to their world in the Nine. He disguises himself and bets they don't has horses as fast as his. Hrungnir who is irritated and intrigued and enthralled, accepts the bet. It's no surprise that Odin leads him on a wild ride-- the giant is bound to lose, no doubt--that will take him to Asgard. Hrungnir was able to recognize who the person was and Odin as well as the gods of other gods offered him a have a drink with them later that night as if to acknowledge his efforts.

Then, Hrungnir, being a massive tyrant, ends in drinking a lot and, in a drunken state, shouts that he'll kill all gods, minus the gorgeous Freya the goddess of Love and Sif, the wife of Thor. Freya continued pouring his drinks, possibly judging the situation correctly. Drinking-related claims are nothing more than empty threats. But, Hrungnir kept on, declaring that he would consume all the ale of gods himself. This, it appears, they were not able to stand for.

Thus, Thor is called in to take down the unruly giant. Thor immediately raises his hammer to kill him. Hrungnir in fear, disguised as bravado, shouts that should Thor be able to kill him with no weapon, Thor would seem a coward to all the world. In order to save his time, the king suggested they join together for a duel.

Thor is, naturally keen to safeguard his name, agrees and they get together in Jotunheim. Hrungnir is covered in stone massive and impressively well-armed. Thor is greeted by a? Bolt of thunder. He throws his hammer at same time Hrungnir throws his whetstone -- a sort of crude sword made from stone. The weapon explodes on contact with Thor's powerful head and sends flint flying across the globe and Thor's hammer smashes the giant on contact. Thor himself will carry a bit of flint that was buried inside his head for the remainder of his life, a reminder of the strength of giants, as well as his own strength.

The lesson to be drawn from this tale that Hrungnir must be destroyed, and not being merely punished or banished due to his transgression being far too severe. He violated the sacredness of Asgard as well as the safety of the gods and goddessesby declaring that he would murder them or break them, in the case in the cases of Freya or Sif. The threat to drink the entire ale of their gods is in violation of one the fundamental values of civilized society: hospitality. In the first place, Hrungnir harangues the gods at their home, a major error. He then takes a swipe at their hospitality. The tale of Hrungnir as well as other tales with giants, illustrates the core principles of Nordic society Chaos and the demise of the core importance of hospitality can't be accepted. The theme which we'll come back in Chapter 16 in which we will focus on the exploits of Beowulf.

Chapter 10: The Mead Of Suttungr: Poetic Inspiration

The Mead of Poetry was a very euphoric drink that Odin later came to own and crave, and then poured it out with a lot of sting It would appear. The tale of the origins of this drink is more fascinating and takes us through a variety of instances and realms of Norse mythology. From malice to murder The Mead of Suttungr transforms and enthrals us in this enchanting, but terrifying story.

The story starts in the middle of a fantastic tale of the connection to two worlds: the Aesir as well as the Vanir. They are the two gods and goddesses that are part of Norse mythology. However, they are the Aesir of Asgard are the most famous. However, the war was started--as many by the Goddess of Love, Freya. At first, she was linked to the Vanir gods and her is a frequent visitor to Asgard as well. Asgardians are so enthralled by them that they even kidnap her. After realizing their love for Freya and her amazing abilities threatened the order of society of

Asgard as a whole, they took the decision to kill her to bring order back. Naturally Vanir Vanir were not pleased with this choice, and there was a war.

After a series of gruelling battles in which the Asgardians utilized conventional weapons, and the Vanir tribe relied on magical methods They decided to call it a truce because they were equally matched. This is how Freya was made an honourary god of the Aesir and the merging of power was recognized. In the aftermath of this agreement, there was an interesting character, Kvasir. The gods and goddesses poured their spittle into a pot to make sure they had kept their word of truce (an old custom that persists to this day, as in the practice of spitting in the palm prior to handshakes on a reputable bet). From their spills, they made Kvasir who was the most knowledgeable person in Midgard and was the best of the wisdom from the gods. There was never any question he could not solve or a problem that you could not resolve.

The talent, of course it was, in turn, was what made Kvasir an extremely valuable commodity and tales of his awe-inspiring knowledge spread throughout the realm of the dwarfs. Therefore, Fjalar and Galar (their names refer to "Deceiver" as well as "Screamer," respectively) invited Kvasir to their house after which they killed him and made mead from the blood of Kvasir. This meant that the mead was believed to have the ability to confer the wisdom of poetry and also poetic ability to anyone who drank it.

However, it was not the only crime that the dwarves were particularly interested in. After their encounter with Kvasir they made the decision to drown the gigantic, Gissing to play sport It would appear. However, Gissing's son Suttungr discovered the crime and pursued the dwarves down, taking the dwarves and chaining several to rocks at low tide. When the tide began to rise and they were swept away, they would drown in a fitting way, which was a fitting punishment. The dwarves begged to save their life, but Suttungr finally relented after the dwarves agreed to grant to him his Mead of Poetry. It is then Suttungr's Mead. Suttungr and he conceals within the mountain, letting his daughter guard it on his behalf.

The mystical substance isn't going to disappear for very long, and Odin discovers this story. Odin's insatiable need for knowledge and insight isn't going to allow the mead to remain undiscovered for too long. Therefore, Odin tricks Suttungr's brother Baugi to help the search by promising to complete the fieldwork on his own, for the duration of a year. When his debt is paid, Odin asks Baugi to go into the mountain on which Suttungr keeps his mead fabled. Baugi obliges but he doesn't have any intent of permitting Odin to take the mead as the wrath of his brother is too much. Therefore, he creates a small hole in the mountain, which is too small for anyone to pass through. But, Odin is quite the fool when he must be, so he transforms his body into snakes, and is able to slip through much to the displeasure of Baugi.

When he is inside, he changes himself into a beautiful young man, to convince Suttungr's daughter of drinking mead. She demands that he spend at least three days with her and then she'll give him three sip of mead. Again, Odin is not one to negotiate So when she brings her to the mead bar, she takes every drop in the fastest way possible. He transforms into an eagle before flying away to Asgard and is followed by Suttungr on the hunt. The gods and goddesses of Asgard are aware of what he's doing and they created an encircling of vessels on the border of Asgard. Odin arrives. Odin is there, and he avoids Suttungr and his gang, he spits out his mead in the vessels waiting for him. There is a legend that says that there are a few drops dispersed all the way to Midgard and serve to inspire the bad poetry and poor research that is written. The effect of the mead is too great to be captured in the smallest drop. Odin will be the person who will ultimately produce

The Mead of Suttungr and it's up to him whether the mead is served to the people he chooses to serve it.

It's quite appropriate it is fitting that Mead of Poetry is in itself a captivating story that is full of excitement, mystery and chaos. The motivation for scholarship and writing isn't easily found as we've all experienced and this tale highlights that only a select few individuals will be granted the benefit from Odin's treasure. This also reveals that, like humankind as a whole, there isn't any character in this story that is innocent or not committing a crime whether through murder or fraud. Another principle that is a part of Norse mythology is the fact that all the creatures of the Nine Worlds are flawed, mortal and capable of causing the greatest harm as well as good. It's all very extremely human.

Chapter 11: Ragnarok: The Nordic Myth It's Not The Movie

The story of Ragnarok, the end of the Norse universe--is based on the fundamental idea of fate: At some unknown time, at the beginning of time, it is believed that the Nine Worlds are fated to come to an end. Ragnarok or "The The Fate of Gods" profoundly affected the way that the Vikings perceived themselves and their place within the global community. When all of existence leads inextricably to an already fated end the perspective of one's life must change. Furthermore to that, as the plot of Ragnarok itself evolves as does the perspective of Nordic the culture.

The tale itself is unbearably dark: A time is coming that it is the Great Winter sweeps over the landscape (one can't imagine not thinking about Game ot Thrones, no?). In the Great Winter, no relief will be available for many seasons There will be no summers to ease the bitter and cold wind of winter. Harvests will cease for years and humanity will be hungry for housing and food that the structure of the universe begins to fall apart. Slaughter will be a common occurrence as fathers and sons as well as daughters and mothers will be battling each other in the chaos and darkness. Morality and laws will fall in this epic struggle to survive.

It's not just the Great Winter fall, but the wolf twins that have chased the moon and the sun for a long time finally, be allowed to hunt their prey. The world will plunge into a never-ending darkness. Yggdrasil which is known as known as the Tree of Life, will begin to shake and the central force that holds the Nine Worlds together will begin to fail. The huge sea serpent Jormungand that is ever-circling Midgard and Midgard, will emerge from deep within the ocean to take on this last of the battles, releasing poisonous venom over the entire earth. Fenrir the wolf-beast of immense size will break his chains before embarking in search of a killer hunt across the land of.

In addition to the supernatural creatures that take over the world in Ragnarok and

Ragnarok, but giants join in the fight too. With their huge boat, Naglfar, they will travel across the world of floods with only Loki the captain. The heavens will be shattered and divided, the fire giants of Muspelheim will be invading as well. Their destruction and chaos will bring down Midgard as they slowly advance towards the Rainbow Bridge in Asgard. This way, order and civilization will be destroyed.

The gods will fight these hordes invading them while being fully aware of their fate lies ahead of them, and there's no way to escape their final destiny. Odin will face Fenrir with all his carefully selected warriors from Valhalla and will defeat. Thor will battle his old foe Jormungand and lose. Although this most powerful of warriors delivers devastating blows to the powerful serpent, he'll be so swollen with the poison of the injured snake that he will die after taking his last nine steps, a remembrance of the final battle of Nine Worlds. Gods Tyr and the Wolf Garm will ultimately kill one another, along with Heimdall as well as Loki, Freyr and the gigantic Surt. So, this massive battle won't just take the lives of those who live in Midgard as well as the rule of the gods of Asgard as well as all the elements of the chaos be defeated. There will be no more. What remains will disappear forever into an endless ocean and nothing but a gap remains. It is like nothing has ever existed.

Although the oldest stories about Ragnarok include this as the ending of the story, or as the ultimate conclusion to everything, some later stories talk about the possibility of regeneration. This is the norm of all mythologies and world religions. Certain gods, such as Thor's sons will endure the destruction and enjoy a happy life with a new, unknown supreme ruler. One person and one woman will be able to survive Midgard by being buried in an old wood before emerging from the chaos to repopulate the area. The dawn will rise from the destruction of the previous. This way The Nine Worlds replenishes a new One World, where no monsters or other supernatural creatures are in the story. This is a stark contrast to the earlier stories of the Apocalypse story.

It's not difficult to speculate on what the reason for the shift could be: The first stories of Ragnarok were a reflection of the old and pagan way of thinking with its origins in thousands and years in Norse culture and theology. As Christianity was introduced to these pagan areas the new worldview was introduced to the defunct Viking culture. It offered hope for hope for redemption and a new beginning, not an end-of-the-world cataclysm. As that influence grew, the narrative of Ragnarok was rewritten slightly. Norse peoples weren't ready to shed their centuries-old beliefs but they did adapt to some of the more recent elements that came from the Christian faith. In the end, the latter would surpass the former and the Vikings entered history when Europe was entering the period of the medieval.

It is important to keep in mind that the first version of Ragnarok - the one with only destruction, death, and void--was perceived in the eyes of Vikings in a manner which is likely to be quite different from the way we think of it today. It's hard to imagine how devastating and utterly absurd life could seem to those peoples if everything they'd ever known, loved or fought for would just be over, with no recall of anything. But, the inevitableness of death for the Vikings was not always awash with the fear and despair that Ragnarok at first evoked. In fact in fact, it promoted a way of thinking about living that accepted death without anxiety, fear, or with dignity. Even gods die, even the giants die, like all human beings pass away. In a world where life was a bit uncertain and there was a constant struggle even during the most prosperous times the idea to death being a welcomed break isn't so unusual. It could even provide a sense of peace and also an excuse for the incredible spirit of bravery and adventure that pervades Viking culture.

Monsters and Heroes

The stories of legends can't be epic when there aren't any heroic foes or great heroes. That's the essence of what myths are constructed from. The stories in all myths tell us what we'd like to become and what we'd like to be--a kind of wish-fulfillment. They describe the world around us as well as the characters that inhabit this world. Heroes and monsters represent the both darkness and light of triumph and defeat both of right-thinking and wrong-doing. We can gain insight into the society that creates these characters, while learning their motivations, values, fears and expectations.

Although monsters can be used in mythology as obstacles for heroes, it's nearly all the time that monsters also serve, symbolically being an image of ourselves. What we are afraid of and hate typically stems from the less powerful demons within our personal natures. In other words, the creatures that are created in mythology symbolize our most feared fears, our hidden desires, or our least positive characteristics. In the ancient mythology the monster usually represents the "other"--she is, or he represents exactly what the author of the story values and believes in. The enemies from Asgard as well as Midgard are the giants, dark and distorted and war-like as well as a myriad of other creatures who work to destroy the balance in the Nine Worlds. Monsters represent chaos, and heroes symbolize order. Yet, monsters can be misread--or, certainly re-interpreted--through time: Loki is both a god and a monster; he can be seen as an evil actor or straight-talking judge. Grendel is the main antagonist in Beowulf has his own story in John Gardner's novel of the same title. The concept of empathy for monsters is something that is happening in the present however it forces us to consider our cultural prejudices.

Heroes are portrayed in a similar way in all mythologies. They must travel, frequently dangerous; on the adventure, the protagonist needs to leave the world of the mundane in which the rules are well-known, to the underworld, a realm of the supernatural or perhaps a faraway country, where the hero must utilize their brains to survive. The hero must face a number of challenges, often with the help of a group of friends and must face the most difficult challenge of all--the ultimate test. If the hero can overcome the challenge, then he/ will receive any kind of reward: Property and wealth; reputation and fame as well as security and friendship. Heroes embody the values the society that tells the story would like us to adhere to whether that's the courage to fight or loyalty to the point of deceit or loyalty to those who they love. Heroes are the absolute illustration of what society is looking for from its most exemplary members. And the ideals of a specific point in the past are often evident by the kind of hero the time has created.

Heroes and monsters speak to our inner psyches. We like to support the good guy , and enjoy the guilt-free triumph of the bad guy. This is among the most enjoyable aspects of mythology, dreaming of being the legendary hero that is admired across the world.

Chapter 12: Trolls: Rock-Dwelling Outsiders

It's a mistake to not include the troll in discussions of the past, culture as well as mythology that is prevalent in the Scandinavian regions and the Scandinavian region, if nothing else then the reality that this word as well as its connotations are now part of our everyday vocabulary. The dolls of the troll were an iconic fashion during the 1960s. Their famous wild hair and bug-like eyes are still well-known and make an appearance in Toy Story 3, as the victims of a runaway train. Trolls are depicted as gentle and mischievous creatures who aid queen Elsa in the hit film Frozen. The word "troll" often and in a casual way to describe somebody who is doing something sinister or unsavory, like in the expression "internet Troll." The creature is a result of Norse mythology, is an object of fascination and infinite interpretation.

The term "troll" could mean any of the creatures and was often used to refer to a giant monster, even a werewolf. As time went on and the legends began to grow and become more believable, the word began in reference to adorable creatures that were not necessarily dangerous but were not particularly dangerous. Unlike giants, trolls weren't in any way a part of the order or order of the world of Midgard They were marginally different from it as they were secluded within their own realms. Later in the mythological stories, it was stated that the trolls refused to accept Christianity which explains the trolls "otherness" in the more civilized spheres of society. This also makes them an enemy of a different type, a threat of a more existential nature; their existence raises questions about the unifying framework of Christianity. Thus, tales of kidnapping--explaining away sudden disappearances of children, especially-- abound.

Trolls usually live in mountains' forests or in caves within mountains. They are described, in the first stories as rather silly and brutish. Maybe not as terrifying as the massive trolls in Harry Potter and the Sorcerer's Stone however they are certainly stupid. The clubs they use have magic powers and can hit the ground to create avalanches and earthquakes. In fact, the troll is a natural phenomenon in many ways: They can transform into stone to hide from detection (what we observe in Frozen) and remain in the woods or caves for a long period of time. The trolls, in essence, do not reside in urban areas, they are utangards, not surrounded by society, and consequently, they pose a threat simply because they're distinct. They protect their territory with a lot of vigilance and that is the reason the stories of fairytale trolls who ask riddles originate You have to solve the question correctly, thus showing your worth before the troll will allow you to pass through the bridge from their world to their world.

Trolls However, they appear easy to fool, and a lot of the stories that tell about their existence are parables of how to deceive the trolling. In one of these stories the story of a boy who needed to find wood in the forest so that his farmer father could pay off his dues. The brothers of his were scared from the forest by a creepy troll however, he set out on himself to find the troll. He carried an uncut block of cheese, which he ate whenever hungry and when the furious troll shook him, he made up the story that the cheese block is actually stone, and squeezed until the whey oozed out. The troll, believing it was a stone was stunned and believed the boy was extremely powerful, and offered to assist the boy cut the wood.

After putting in so much effort cutting timber, the troll invited the boy into his home to eat dinner. While the troll was making the food, he enlisted the boy to go get some water. As the boy looked at two huge buckets it was clear that there was no way they would be strong enough to transport these buckets back, and especially those that were filled with water. He wanted the troll to realize that his strength was actually an illusion. Therefore, he offered to collect his entire stream for the Troll, and return it to the home. The troll obviously didn't want an entire spring within his home, therefore he instructed the boy to tend to the fire while he collected the water. So, the boy's claim to be strong was unquestioned.

After the two of them were seated to eat their breakfast, the boy challenged the troll in an eating contest. He put his knapsack in under his shirt and, pretended to be eating it, stuffed the knapsack up with porridge. After the sack was full and he was able to sneakily cut an opening in the sack and continued to pretend to eat, while the porridge dripped from the hole in his stomach. When the troll was fully stuffed but was unable to accept defeat the boy suggested that to cut a hole into his stomach too. The troll did what the boy had suggested and, of course the self-inflicted wound proved fatal. The boy then helped himself to the treasure of the troll of precious metals before returning to his home and his father was able to repay his debt.

Apart from being outwitted Trolls were also terrified by lightning and thunder, which, of course was the symbol of Thor. They were also terrified when they heard church bells. Their disdain for Christianity is what makes them fearful and sceptical towards the Christian church. Based on the previous story the majority of stories about trolls are actually tales of creativity and the importance of being quick with your sense of humor. Some stories focused on staying at home, and being protected from the standards of civilization and the polite society.

Chapter 13: Valkyries: Friendly Spirits Or Fiendish Sprites?

The Valkyries have been portrayed in both ancient Norse stories as well as in contemporary depictions, as friendly but fierce, aids to Odin during battle as well as in battle. They have been characterized as strong, beautiful women who come swooping down onto a battlefield--sometimes flying, sometimes on mounted horseback--to take the worthy dead back to Valhalla. Sometimes, they are even depicted as warriors on their own and were famous in their relationships with mortal males. There is however an older source depicting a darker version of female characters, whose power may not always be admirable.

In fact, the word "Valkyrie" is essentially "choosers of the dead," implying that they are directly associated with Odin when deciding who to take back to Valhalla to him. Some older texts also refer to the idea that Valkyries played a key role in deciding the ones who would die, and not just those who were returned to Valhalla which is why their role in the field can be considered threatening and even threatening to certain. In one tale in which the Valkyries are shown in the midst of a battle on a loom, where they weave the destiny of the warriors who will be fighting: They weave their thread out from stomach contents, while heads that have been cut off serve as weights and swords serve as beaters.

They are singing in apparent joy about the upcoming slaughterwhich is not the image of a the divine assistance.

The concept of the Valkyrie is not exclusive in Nordic literature, neither. There were strong female characters in Celtic legends (the banshee for instance) and other pre-Christian mythological and religious texts. Females as harbingers for doom are often featured in a variety of mythological stories from the past.

In the Viking time period, Valkyries were an integral part of the battlefield of history and legend. Women's amulets adorned with long gowns with hair pulled back, adorned with drinking horns have been found in a variety of burial locations. It is believed that they represent some kind of protection. In fact it was during period of the Vikings that the rather sinister earlier version of the Valkyrie have been replaced by an amiable, more glamorous image. The Vikings required Valkyries to serve as a source of help when they endured the constant battles and raids.

A few years ago archaeologists discovered a figure in Denmark which appeared to date at least 800 CE, the dawn of the Viking age. It was of a woman who carried the shield and sword. It was evident that she was female, since hair was long and put into a ponytail and she was wearing the form of a dress, which was topped by an apron. It is probable that the statue was a luck-in-the-air gift for an incoming Viking set to embark on a journey.

Historical researchers have also found runic inscriptions which mention Valkyries. Valkyries located in Sweden. One of them appears to be a sad love poem, in which the author speaks of the Valkyrie's "wolfish sexual perversion" along with "unbearable desire" The poem is in line with the current perception of the Valkyrie as stunningly beautiful, yet distinctly alien. Consider the veela animals in Harry Potter and the Goblet of Fire. While the movie doesn't reveal their fierceness but the book definitely emphasizes it. These beautiful women can display incredible force when they are pushed.

Women resembling Valkyrie are also seen in England as well as other Anglo-Saxon countries, suggesting the traditional Norse use of the word became a major element of Germanic mythologies, too. These strong floating "victory women" are mentioned in a few Old English texts, for instance in the text Charms to Stop the Pain:

They were very loud, yes,

as they rode across their (burial) burial mound

They were fierce when they ran across landscape.

Protect yourself today, you are able to get through this tumult.

Out Little spear, if there's one in the.

It was situated behind lime-wood with a light-weighted shield

where these mighty women harnessed their power, and then sent the spears with a roar.

There are theories suggesting that suggest these mythological figures originate from specific and real rituals which were practiced during the period during the Vikings and prior to. Women played the role of quasi-shamans at the time of ceremonies of sacrifice to the gods and burial. It doesn't be a huge leap to associate these women with the dead of war and the choice of the deceased.

The transition from the ghoulish ghosts to beautiful women who wore shields occurred in the age of the Vikings. In fact, the concept of Valhalla changed in stories of the period. Before the Vikings, Valhalla had been an unsettling place, a battlefield in itself, where warriors killed were destined to endure the battleground for the rest of their lives. When the Vikings were the dominant cultural power within the Nordic areas, Valhalla became a warrior's paradise, featuring competitions and sparring, that were followed by endless drinking and feasting. It was also the moment that the Valkyries became Odin's aids, carrying fatally wounded soldiers through the doors of Asgard and into Odin's magnificent hall. The goddess Freya is closely associated with the Valkyries in that she takes fallen warriors out of battle into her Hall, Folkvang. Folkvang is the hall where fallen warriors are escorted. Valkyries' destiny, according to their legend is inseparable from the fate of their warriors that they guard--the Vikings.

Chapter 14: Elves And Dwarves: Creatures Of The Sky And Earth

Norse mythology also has a lot of characters with dwarves and elves, which can be positive or negative depending on the situation. It is evident that a lot of the modern fantasy world originates of this Norse worldview. Tolkien's works, Dungeons and Dragons, Game of Thrones, just to mention a few examples which owe a lot to the ideas of Viking warriors as well as supernatural beings. Dwarves and elves aren't exclusive to Norse mythology, naturally however they are an integral part of the mythology of the Nine Worlds, and their modern depiction is more closely linked to Nordic mythology than the rest of.

The elves are frequently depicted as gorgeous creatures, appearing to shine from within, like Cate Blanchett and Liv Tyler in Lord of the Rings. They are closely linked to the gods, specifically those belonging to the Vanir branch of gods and goddesses who utilize magic as a part of their abilities. They are also known as the Aesir section from Asgard will be more familiar to the modern world, since the Vikings became the mainstay of Norse culture prior to when Christianity arrived. The Aesir branch is not dependent more on magic than it does on the skills of warriors and formidable weapons. Hence they are more appropriate to the Viking mythology.

In all likelihood the elves were portrayed as sky-based creatures and the distinction between the elves as well as the gods were not clear, however, it was evident that they were a distinct class of the animal. Their relationship with humans however were at best ambivalent. The elves are not kind creatures overall however, and even though they do make mistakes, they are more of a sly kind--they're certainly not Harry Potter house elves, with their largely subservient nature and jolly good humor. In particular there was the belief that elves were responsible for the development of grave human ailments, but they also help with ailments however only if you offer an adequate reward to compensate.

Humans also had the ability to be bred with elves it was believed, consequently, strange or impish children were generally believed to be half-elves. There are , of obviously stories, several fairy tales. stories. The Brothers Grimm, for one that is a part from the Germanic tradition. It is also closely linked to Scandinavian stories of elves abducting children.

Yet reverence for elves lasted throughout the centuries and was often interspersed in worship to the ancestors of one's. It was believed that humans could be transformed into elves once they died therefore, these two kinds of worship were interspersed. Evidence suggests how the deity worshipped by elves continued even after Christianity was the dominant culture within the region. In this way one could say that the elves trumped the gods.

The opposite to the elf's elf's dwarf is. Instead of being a glowing creature from the sky, dwarfs are swarthy beasts of the underground. Their underground dwelling,

Svartalfheim, is a maze of mines and forges. The dwarfs were celebrated for their metal-working talents. They are often depicted as dark, and sometimes black creatures, in old stories, there's no mention of their short stature. This relationship was introduced during the modern age. In some cases, they're known as "dark Elves," adding to their unique relationship with the beings of the night.

The dwarves are famous for their skill as smiths. some of the most important totems of Norse mythology were actually born from the dwarf workshops one of the most famous of which is Thor's hammer Mjollnir. Additionally, they created Odin's legendary spear, Freyr's ship , which always enjoys a pleasant wind as well as the chain that binds the great wolf Fenrir which eventually killed Odin in Ragnarok. They also are responsible for forming the long , golden hair of Thor's wife Sif. It is fascinating that dwarfs, not the gods or goddesses, are the ones responsible for creating many of the iconic objects which are commonplace in Norse mythology. The distinctions that separate supernatural entities of all nature are usually blurred but the dwarven heritage is one of immense strength and wisdom.

They are also known for their power. In reality, the dwarfs are the ones who hold up the sky, which is a strange task for those who live underground However, it's there however. Austri, Vestri, Nordri and Sudri represent the four areas of the sky. their names, as ought to be obvious, correspond to east, west northand south.

In the myths about the Elves, dwarves are often described as deceased humans. The concept of the afterlife is a central theme in Norse mythology can be described as a vague and baffling thing, unlike like Egyptian mythology, where the afterlife is an ongoing obsession, with the sole only exception being Valhalla. It is also because the Vikings were able to symbolize the entirety of Norse culture towards the end of their pagan times and the mythologies that have survived and passed down to us are heavily in the direction of the Vikings. So, the dead ancestors of the past were worshipped as they were either as elves or dwarves. Their afterlife included not only Valhalla as well as Freya's Hall Folkvang, Hel's world in the Underworld as well as many different possible places.

There are other creatures in Norse mythology aside from elves or Dwarves, for sure. We've reviewed a few of the most well-known gods and goddesses, witnessed how the gigantics fought each other and experienced how powerful Jormungand, the Sea Serpent. Land spirits also exist that were equally significant to the Germanic peoples as were the elves, and were worshiped long before the advent of Christianity. It's no surprise, when you consider that land spirits could bring blessings or curses during an adventure through the harsh northern landscape. There is the Norn, an ancient tribe of gods that dispense out fates, like Ragnarok. There is also the Disir the Disir, a cult of female spirits that alternate between a semblance to the Valkyries and the Elves. In reality, the ancient Norse texts are filled with amazing and intriguing creatures that come in all sizes, shapes and abilities. The characters is only among the numerous delights of reading these classic texts.

Chapter 15: Midgard And The Humans

The idea of "Nine Worlds" is sometimes a bit unclear, particularly when it appears that all the creatures of the other worlds move around in Midgard, the one which is home to humans, us. We must remember, however as with all the antiquated civilizations and cultures, the realm which is inhabited by humans remains limited to the area that is inhabited by "humans similar to us." This means that with limited mobility and technology and the notion of the whole earth was not an option Civilization was confined to the particular culture you lived and the beliefs you adhered to. However, even as the Vikings explored out beyond their territorial borders, the people they encountered and were "other," and thus weren't as human in the same manner. This isn't unique to Norse mythology, but it is a common theme in all mythological systems from the preindustrial era (in the same way as different civilizations from that of the Celtic through that of Egyptian as well as the Chinese and on). Therefore, Midgard is where the Norse people resided and settled. It was the place they settled It is the only visible world in the Nine Worlds.

The term "Midgard" refers to, in essence, "middle enclosure", which places it at the very center of the universe--this is the most civilized area of the planet--and located in "the in the middle of" the unexplored world. Therefore, Midgard is two concepts simultaneously: It's an adjective of comfort as well as of elevation--we're the central point of the universe, and an expression that creates fears and feelings of insecurity. Midgard is located in the middle of real and metaphysical threats which range that range from Jormungand The sea serpent which encircles Midgard as well as the forces of foreigners, such as Christian conversions, and Arab traders. This is in reference to the key notions of utangard and innangard--that can be described as "inside of the boundary" as opposed to what lies "outside of the boundary." Midgard is very much innangard, whereas other peoples and cultures, as well as certain of the other Nine Worlds (Jotunheim--land of giants) are utangard in a large sense.

Because Midgard employs "gard" instead of "heim "--"gard" being the closest thing to fencing or enclosure and fences, while "heim" is a reference to the concept of home, Midgard is more in the spirit of Asgard as opposed to Jotunheim. Asgard is the ideal location for peace, security and civilisation. Midgard is the middle ground which aspires to the Asgard level. Yet, Midgard, like Asgard is likely to be a place of chaos and destruction in Ragnarok.

The myths depict Midgard as having been created out of the corpse of the gigantic Ymir who was killed by gods. A fence was constructed using Ymir's eyebrows ensure the safety of Midgard from unruly outsiders. This gesture of symbolic significance was made in the real world of times when every farmer constructed the fence around their farm: Every Norse farm or area was a miniature representation of Midgard in itself. Hearth and home are featured prominently in mythology, and even in the midst of all the Viking adventures. In fact it was the desire to protect the hearth and home that inspired the Vikings into raids and into combat.

In other places within the book, people of Midgard - that is the Norse people who practiced the pagan worldview about their gods using extremely anthropomorphic manners. The gods behaved in a similar way to the humans do and the reverse is also true. Therefore, the connection between the people in Midgard with the gods and humans of Asgard is close. In Greco-Roman mythology gods were involved in human affairs and interacted around in them as they pleased. Sometimes, this was due to the desire to please a gorgeous young woman, for example. However, it was also motivated by an enticement from God to safeguard Midgard. Thor particularly was charged with guarding Midgard's inhabitants, a task that has been happily filled through Thor in the Marvel Universe of Avengers movies.

The relationship also took on the form of worship that was reciprocal. When people desired something from gods, they offered them offerings or gifts in hopes of receiving something in the return. The ideal model for this, naturally is a very anthropocentric one, and was resonated across Viking culture. The chieftain of one particular clan was likely to have an entanglement with his warriors exactly like the way they imagined that the relation between gods from Asgard and the human race of Midgard was to be. A warrior who stood up for the chieftain was entitled to the full amount of profits of battle. The chieftain for his part, was under as a duty to his warriors to select battles with care, plan his strategy and guard the warrior as best possible. This kind of reciprocity was the standard of society at the time and it's no surprise that it is reflected in our interactions with the gods.

The obligation of warriors and their chieftains was mirrored in that of Midgard as well as Asgard in different ways and. Chieftains might expect - just as Odin would expect from his Valhalla companion that a warrior would prefer to sacrifice their lives in combat for the sake of honor, and not fight against unpredictability. Chieftains could also be able to expect that, if they didn't respect the warrior by giving them fair share and respect, the warrior may leave to join another chieftain. This was akin with humans and their gods If a god or goddess seemed to fail a household or village, the allegiance of the gods could be transferred to another god who could provide them with more wealth.

The relationship was reshaped with changes in Christianization of Viking the territory. The chieftains were crowned kings and warriors became serfs and knights who pledged their loyalty to the king forever. This was echoed by the new-found relationship between humans as well as the Christian God The absolute obedience and a complete faith were the prerequisites to save oneself. Furthermore, the familiar gods and goddesses that were human-like changed to an unfathomable and all-knowing Creator. Consequently the relationship between them grew less distant, as was the relation between the king and his people. The concept about Midgard itself was made more complex by the age of exploration and discovery of other cultures and ways of living. The Vikings kept to this idea for a longer time than most other pagan communities that were around at the time. Maybe because of this, Norse mythology has an incredible way of being incorporated into contemporary entertainment over and over again.

Chapter 16: Beowulf The Dark Twilight Of Norse Mythology And Early Christianity

Then, we discover the story of Beowulf, possibly an unorthodox addition to the long tale of Norse mythology and culture. Beowulf has, for numerous convincing reasons, become accepted by literary critics as the first genuine literary work in English literature, despite the fact that there are two major issues with this assimilation. It is first composed in the language is referred to as "Old English," but that language has more resemblances to German than contemporary English (remember that the Anglo-Saxons are Germanic tribes) and secondly, it is about the heroic adventures that were the work of Scandinavian heroes, such as the Spear-Danes as well as The Geats (or Germanic Goths) as well as the Swedes. Therefore, Beowulf is right at right at home in the pantheon of Viking mythology and culture, even though it's an older work the fact is that it was recorded between the 8th and 10th centuries. This was during the peak of both Viking civilization as well as the beginning of

Christian change in the north of Europe. Because of this interplay between the ancient and the modern in terms of culture, "Beowulf" the character represents the ideals and qualities of a legendary Viking warrior and warrior, while Beowulf is often a story of God and the rewards He bestows.

Beowulf is, as with many other fantastic tales of legends is told in three parts. The first is that Beowulf the Geat is required to lend his assistance for Hrothgar the Spear-Dane to confront the demon-creature Grendel. He must then confront Grendel's vile mother, who is furious at her. Then be an elderly man take on the dragon who is trying to destroy his home.

It may at first appear odd to think that Beowulf is able to travel across the world to be a king from a different country However, it is evident from the beginning that his motives are valid and have two facets. In the first place, there is a reference to a previous relationship between his father and Hrothgar and the fact which suggests that Hrothgar was the one who repaid his debt. It is the second reason that drives Beowulf throughout the story: Beowulf seeks eternal glory and fame for the rest of his life. He is the most famous hero of his time. The poem itself says, "he was the mightiest man on earth, strong and born." Why do he want to be more famous? to cement his name throughout the centuries: Grendel is a villain unlike anything anyone has before seen, and so Beowulf's victory over the demon will be heard across the globe.

The current situation is grave the situation is dire. King Hrothgar has built the grand Hall, Heorot following many productive decades of leading soldiers to battle, of capturing and consolidating power and wealth. Heorot is the final gift he gives to his soldiers and himself -- a shining beacon of civilization and light in a world of war. It is indeed a stunning hall brimming with treasures and mead. However, without warning Grendel the demon-creature is able to attack the hall at any time and sneaks in at night to slaughter people, then taking them back to his abode for the purpose of butchering (it is revealed that he's a cannibal). Grendel's motives, as described in this poem, which dates from before psychology, are ambiguous. Two theories are offered to explain the root of Grendel's plight The second is pure jealousy and straightforward; Grendel was a rejected and being an "other," and when Grendel hears the music and laughter in the hall, paired with its extravagant presentation of money, he snaps at the crowd and seeks revenge with a murderous intent. The second reason--which is probably an ulterior motive thrown in from the monks-scribes that recorded the story as oral--is that Grendel is a creature that is not worthy of Christian salvation. And when Grendel hears the people in the hall ranting about God and His blessings his first instinct is to kill them.

The hall was mostly empty prior to the arrival of Beowulf, but Beowulf is now there with his men as well as the brave Hrothgar's cohorts. At night, while they're sleeping Grendel appears and begins to brutally attack the warriors who are asleep. Beowulf gets into action and literally tears Grendel's arm from his body. They hang it on the ceiling of the hall, a kind of horrific trophy. Grendel walks back to his cave, badly wounded.

Although there is plenty of talk about the great achievement of Beowulf, as well as a few remark about other epic battles from the past The hall isn't yet completely safe. In the midst of darkness, Grendel's mom arrives to exact revenge, and to take her son's arm. Beowulf is unable to let the prize disappear, and so tracks his mother back to her cave and shows a superhuman amount of strength and endurance when it comes to killing her. First, his sword isn't strong enough to defeat the demon-mother which is why he has to take her out of her arms and knock her down with her weapon, believed to be too heavy for mortals to carry. In addition, the lair hidden deep beneath the marshlands and, therefore, Beowulf must keep his breath for an inhuman amount time to reach it and return. When he arrives after his return, he's not empty handed. He slits off Grendel's head, which is atypically big--and is able to swim back to it, showing that Grendel is gone one and for all.

It is apparent that Grendel -- and as a result, his mother, has committed the greatest sin in the present time Grendel has violated the hospitality rules. This isn't just because the people he kills are killed; in the time of constant war killing warriors was not a common occasion. But he also enters the space of civilisation and takes away the peace of the hearth and home which the legendary warrior Hrothgar was so determined to attain. Beowulf is, on the other hand is not just rid the realm of the scourge of Grendel He has also brought back the right and proper order of things actions.

The final battle of Beowulf will be held in his home country 50 years after his crowning as the king of his home country and his splendor is recognized throughout his Scandinavian world. A dragon's hoard is perturbed by a small-time thief and the dragon leaps down and sets fire on Beowulf's realm.

In this stage of the story's narrative, meanings change: Beowulf is not looking for fame or treasure. In fact the treasure starts to look like little more than dragon fodder, a massive horde of creatures that are ungodly. In addition, the emphasis on the most Viking of customs, wyrd, or fate, begins to creep into. It is clear that Beowulf's fate lies with that of the dragon. taking down the dragon, he's definitely doomed to be killed. When Beowulf is able to deliver the fatal blow of the sword into the dragon's stomach and the dragon puts his teeth into the neck of Beowulf. The poison is sure to cause death to him.

The final scenes featuring the legendary hero Beowulf are elegiac in their tone and signal the end of the phase of Viking civilization. Of course, the poem was composed much from those (mythological) events itself by those who were responsible for the demise of this world. Beowulf is looking at the wealth which he has found and he does not take pleasure in it and neither does he find any comfort from his illustrious profession and fame. Instead, he expresses gratitude to the Almighty in what is the end of himself and his style of living. It is clear that the Christianization of Viking culture is total. He is honored in the following manner:

"They claimed that they were the most powerful of the kings on planet

He was the person who was most gentle and fair-minded.

Most kind to his fellow citizens and eager to be famous."

Chapter 17: Additional Enchanting Stories And Figures

One can imagine, this collection of tales has only scratched the surface of what's found to us in our canon of Norse stories and myths. Keep in mind this: the Norse peoples covered a huge geographical area and encompassed numerous cultures, which is why there are countless legends and stories of the gods and heroes of the world gods, goddesses and enchantresses creatures and enemies. Norse mythology can be seen to resonate across the world even to this day as we've witnessed the influence of Norse mythology on popular culture in a variety of ways, both large and small.

While we've encountered some of the most well-known gods and goddesses but there are many others that make up the Norse pantheon. Below are some additional examples.

* Goddess Frigg has been identified as the spouse of Odin However, her characteristics

aren't very clear and she's quite similar to Freya, the goddess. Freya

* Heimdall is the god of protection of Asgard and has a supernaturally sharp hearing and vision

The God Tyr is the god who oversees not just battle, but also the law and justice. Although there isn't much that exists from the Viking time period about him There are some sources that suggest that he is an older god that was revered by many Germanic tribes

* Bragi is the bard from Valhalla who plays his songs and singing his poetry There are some reports that say Bragi is the spouse of Idun who protects the golden apples

* Vili and Ve are Odin's unspoken brothers who are believed to have played a role in the development of the universe, but are given little credit

In terms of stories most of the important stories are told at least partially or at least in some form within this book. There are several other intriguing tales like the defense of Asgard and the way the gods construct a formidable wall to defend their homes (this is certainly in line with The Game of Thrones series, one might imagine). There are more tales of the adventures of Fenrir, the legendary wolf that turns out to be the cause of Odin's end, and Jormungard who plays the same function for Thor. There are many stories concerning Thor's exploits as a trickster as well as a warrior, and Loki's various adventures. A lot of these stories are interspersed with the most important ones, and reveal the traits of gods and goddesses through the same ways which we have explored in the initial chapters.

Since the monsters and heroes can be, for vast part, gods as well as other gods who reside within the Nine Worlds, we have previously explored the characters that have the greatest significance to the mythological realm in Norse culture. The giants themselves are so significant in their many exploits that you could compose a collection of tales specifically for the giants.

The impact that Norse mythology has been able to have over popular culture was massive from comics to films and television, as well as music and video games. A number of the most significant examples have been previously mentioned in this text. Naturally, this is not the only one. Marvel Comics Universe and the films it has inspired have been hugely successful and extremely popular: Thor is a character that appears throughout the Avengers films and stories, and the mythology of Norse mythology is discussed in greater detail (if not always accurately) in the stand-alone films in which Thor becomes the main character, such as, Thor: The Dark World and Thor: Ragnarok. Animation films like How to Train Your Dragon and its sequels rely heavily on stereotypes of what are the Vikings were. In addition, there are aspects of Norse mythology in the mega-hit film Frozen that is based upon a tale written by Hans Christian Andersen, the Danish writer.

It's not extravagant to suggest that nearly every aspect of what we've come across as"the "fantasy" genre of our times has been influenced to a certain extent from Norse mythology and the culture. The many mentions of Game of Thrones throughout the text are only one example. Also, there is The Lord of the Rings franchise which comprises both J.R.R. Tolkien's novels and the five recent films based on the books. The elves and dwarfs feature prominently they're turned into heroes, even if hobbits are invented by The English writer. In the book, English comedian Douglas Adams also featured Odin and Thor in his Hitchhiker's guide to the Galaxy trilogy and more so throughout the Dirk Gently detective books, including The Long Dark Tea-Time of the Soul. The Newberry award-winning author, Nancy Farmer, borrowed from Norse mythology in her 2004 book Sea of Trolls.

Norse heroes and gods are frequently featured in a myriad of science fiction themed shows, including Stargate SG-1 and Doctor Who. We should not overlook the cult cartoon series from the 1980scalled He-Man and Masters of the Universe, had many elements taken from Norse mythology and culture.

And lastly, who can not remember Led Zeppelin's many music tributes to Norse Cosmology? Their inspiration comes from Tolkien's novels and his series and are incredibly powerfully evocations of a dark and dangerous world that is full of excitement and ready for telling.

Chapter 18: The Aesir Gods As Well As Goddesses

Odin

Odin is the Odin is the king of Odin, the king of all Aesir gods and the ruler of Asgard. He is known under a myriad of names, including Gangleri, Odinn, Othinn, Vak, and Valtam. Odin is also known as the Allfather is the God of War, Death and Knowledge.

He also has a connection to the Gallows, healing, magic poetry, royalty, sorcery, shamanism as well as the alphabet of runic. Wednesday comes by his surname (Woden's Day).

Odin is the name given to Odin by Borr as well as Bestla. Borr was the child of Buri who was the very first Norse god, while Bestla was the child of the huge Bolthorn. Buri was born by the time that the cow Audhumbla consumed the icy, salty Ginnungagap while she fed Ymir the first giant of frost.

The All-knowing Godfather has been married to Frigg however the couple also had a romantic relationship and a romance with Freya and Rind as well as other. Odin was the father of Baldr, Hodr and Hermod with Frigg while he also had Thor with Jord along with Vidar and Grid Grid. Odin is the dad of Vidarr as well as Vali. According to another version (by Snorri Sturluson), Odin is also the father of Bragi and Heimdallr. Hod and Tyr but other versions claim that they, especially Tyr were bred by someone else.

Odin also established a variety in royal lineages through his sons Sigi (Volsungs),Skjold (Denmark's Skjolding dynasty), Yngvi (Swedish Ynglings) as well as Saeming (a branch of Norwegian King Saeming).

The god of Asgard is described as a one-eyed long-bearded god , who wears large-brimmed hat which allows him to travel around the world and not be identified. There are two ravens and two wolves as pets. Huginn (thought) as well as Munnin (memory) (memory) two ravens, were assigned to keep Odin informed by flying around the globe and providing him with information.

Another reason is that Odin is an expert in his field and is well-versed in military tactics and other such strategies. His wolf friends comprised Geri as well as Freki. Odin rides Sleipnir which is a horse with eight legs, in fight and is connected to the berserkers the warriors who are who are known for their combat techniques and wearing bear or wolf skins.

Odin is missing an eye This is the reason Odin is usually depicted with one eye patch one eye closed. The journey to Yggdrasil The World Tree, cost him one eye. The desire to go into the tree caused him to stab himself with his spear, and then hang from the tree.

He endured nine nights and days hanging on the Yggdrasil before being finally permitted to peek at the trees. Odin noticed mystic symbols appearing on the rocks beneath his feet. His strength enabled him to move the rocks up and observe the runes that were magical. After seeing these symbols Odin felt free of any burdens and felt energized.

The Allfather was able to drop gently from the tree and safely and fall to earth. Allfather Allfather was then in a position to drink of the (Talking Head) Mimir's Well of Wisdom. The well lets to allow the Dew of Knowledge to seep into it.

Odin had to give up his sight for Mimir to gain the opportunity to drink his water, and to gain huge knowledge. Odin's missing eye is in a secret location that just Mimir can see. Mimir makes use of Odin's eye to see far and distant events, which it allows Odin, the Lord of Asgard to see further ahead. In the war of the Aesir Vanir, Mimir suffered death and then beheaded. Odin took Mimir's head and consults it for guidance.

Odin is famous for his ability to speak only in poetry. This is the reason for Odin's connection to poetry. He was born with the ability following the taking the mead of poetics from giants. The giant Suttung took possession to the mead poetry when he saved the lives the dwarfs Fjalar as well as Galar who were the ones responsible for killing his father Gilling and his mother.

The two dwarves who murdered each other brewed poetry out of the blood of the humans Kvasir that was formed out of the spits of gods and goddesses when the conflict among Aesir and Vanir came to an end in a peace. The most wise man on Midgard was enticed by the Dwarves to their home and was killed.

The mead of poetics provided those who drank of it with an infinite amount of wisdom as well as the ability to compose and deliver poetically beautiful words. Odin who was always looking for ways to become the most intelligent dressed himself up as a farmer called Bolverkr to be close to Baugi the brother of Suttung. He caused the nine farmhands of Baugi to kill one another and then presented him to Baugi in exchange for serve as an employee in exchange for sipping of the mead that was owned by Baugi's brother.

Baugi, despite being uneasy, agreed to Bolverkr's offer. When the farmer was done working in the field, he took the farmer on a trip to Suttung who refused to comply with the God's suggestion to take drinking a glass of mead. Not willing to give up, Odin was able to get into the home of Gunnlod's sister Suttung who was charged with protecting the mead's magical properties and with the assistance of Baugi.

Odin changed into a handsome young man who seduced Gunnlod. He promised to be a bed in the giantess's bed for 3 nights for three drinks from the mead. He emptyed three vats of mead, and returned to Asgard. Odin keeps the mead (or handed it over to Bragi, his Bragi, his son Bragi) since the time he was a child and has been rewarded deserving people (the poets and scholars) with knowledge out of the mead.

It is believed that the Allfather Also, he is the head of Valhalla Valhalla, the magnificent home of the dead. It is also where Valkyries carry the majority of warriors killed in battle, who are worthy of entering Valhalla.

The ones who weren't selected are taken in by Freya and sent to Folkvangr. Odin is well-known for raising and communicating with the dead with the purpose of learning their wisdom. He also brought the top fighters to battle him in the battle of Ragnarok.

Odin was one of gods that lost their lives in the "Batlle of the Gods Doomed" according to the prophecy of Ragnarok.

Frigg

Frigg Also known as Fija, Frea, Frija, Frige, Frigga and Friggja was the spouse of Odin and is the most powerful female god. Frigg is the goddess of marriage, fertility and Childbirth as well as Love.

The goddess of power is connected to the management of household affairs, motherhood, spinning and weaving. She is seated with Odin on the top seat of Hlioskjalf in which she is able to see all the realms. Frigg is a resident of Fensalir (wetland Halls) within Asgard. She was the daughter of Fjorgynn the male version of Earth. It is Friday (Frige's day) is named for her. It is common to confuse her with goddess Freya and many scholars have suggested that the two are in fact linked and could be one and the same thing.

Frigg is believed to be the one who created clouds, as she weaved them out of strings of destiny or Wyrd. She is also able to see into the future, but does not reveal her visions to anyone.

She is frequently usually accompanied by Gna who serves as her agent. Gna is believed to have had relationships and affairs with Ve and Vili and rode on Hofvarpnir on her journeys. Frigga is also frequently with the gods Fulla, Hlin, and Lofn.

Frigga is well-known for her efforts to stop his death. Balder. She made all objects in nature promise to never hurt her son by using Odin. But she believed that the tiny mistletoe was tiny, and that's why she did not attempt to get it to swear the oath. Loki got his way to being aware of the weakness that was Balder and was the reason for his demise.

Frigga is an adept of seidr, an ancient type that is a form of Norse magic. This is the reason why she's often depicted in the form of a volva by Vikings. This power lets Frigg to change the fate of every being. This means that the goddess of power does not just know the fate of all creatures, but she can also alter their destiny should she wish to.

The goddess has in her belongings is an assortment of of falcon feathers that can be used to alter her appearance. Similar to Freya's hawk feathers that Loki employed to change shape on to get from the wrath of Idunn.

THOR

It is believed that the Norse God of War Thor is also known as Porr, Thunor, and Donner. The god of war is the son of Odin and the goddess of earth Jord. The known as Defender for Both Asgard as well as Midgard is often referred to by the name of God of Thunder and is sometimes referred to called the God of Thunderstorms.

Thor is tied to Sif The Goddess of fertility. But, Thor bore sons Magni (Strong), Modi (Angry) and daughter Thrud (Strength) in their union to the gigantic Jarnsaxa which is known as known as the "iron cutting-edge". Thor's hall is referred to as Bilskirnir located in Thrudheim the region that is called "place of strength". Thursday is named for him.

Thor is believed to be the god of thunder. He sits over the skies and control the weather and the wind, aside from thunder and lightning. Thor is also associated with storms fair weather and strength, crop, oak trees and healing, consecration and fertility. As per Adam of Bremen who was the Christian missionary who went to Thor's temple in Uppsala the locals would pour brew into the temple and pour it onto the form of Thor within the temple. It was common practice to make a wish for the god in time of plagues and famines.

Thor is a horse drawn by two goats Tanngniost (tooth grinder) and Tanngrisnir (gap-tooth). Thor, the God of Thunder is often joined by Thialfi, who is the messenger of the gods as well as the god's sister Roskva.

The brothers became Thor's servants following Thialfi caused one goat to be disabled in its leg. Thor and Loki had a night at the farmstead of the sibling. Thor lets the family of the farmer to eat the goat's flesh. However, Thialfi sucked the marrow out of a leg bone.

In the time that God of Thunder granted life for his animals, one was weak on the leg. In order to placate God's anger, Thialfi as well as Roskva were made his service animals.

Thor's weapon of choice is a hammer called Mjolnir. The hammer was given to him by the brothers of dwarfs Brok as well as Eitri. When the ancient Nordics were hit by a storm they believed that god was riding his chariot. Lightning appeared when Thor was throwing Mjolnir.

Thor, the much-loved Thor has been described as being a muscular being. His belt known as Megingjard which increases his strength by a lot. He also wears iron gloves that enable the wearer to grip Mjolnir.

The gloves also let the hammer fly back toward the man. Thor is usually red haired, but in comic books the character is shown as blonde. Thor is played by actor Chris Hemsworth, a blonde actor as part of Thor and Avengers. Thor and Avengers film series by Marvel.

Although he is a for his hotheadness, Thor continues to be a favorite with humans, not just because he protects them and protector, but also because he never demanded sacrifices of human beings in his honor. He directed his anger especially when he loses anger, towards the giants. This was done through smashing heads giants by using

Mjolnir which, in turn, means "that that smashes".

Thor had a time when he lost his hammer and caused immense sorrow. He woke one day to discover Mjolnir missing. Thor confessed his feelings to Loki who accompanied the other to Freya. After arriving, Thor and Loki borrowed her feather robe that goddess offered without hesitation.

Loki flew into the land of the giants with Freya's feathers, and encountered Thrym. He was the King of race of giants Thurse confessed to stealing Mjolnir. Thyrm hidden it in the depths of eight leagues and promised to return it in the event that Freya is willing to be married by him. Loki returns with the story.

Thor advised Freya to dress in bridal gowns and travel with him to the giants' land, however, the goddess resisted. The jewelry of Brisings to fall apart. The gods gathered to determine how to bring Mjolnir back. Heimdall advised that Thor wear wedding gowns, a necklace of Brisings and keys of a housewife and wedding jewels.

While hesitant, Thor agreed in order to stop any attempt to take over the giants. Thor and Loki who was disguised as servant and went for a meeting with the gigantics. They were served a meal in which the gods disguised took in a great deal of food and consumed plenty of mead.

Thrym observed and exclaimed that the fact that he'd never seen an elopement bride who ate that much or looked as terrifying. Thor explained to the effect that this "goddess" seemed so excited to travel to the Land of the Giants that "she" hasn't had a meal or slept for the past eight nights.

Thrym was Mjolnir moved forward and placed on the god's lap in order to begin the wedding. The giants were shocked when Thor was revealed to them. Thrym was the first one to be slain by the power of Thor and the Hammer. The kin of the King were also killed.

According to Volva, Thor perished during his battle against the snake Jormungand at the time of Ragnarok. The deceased seeress predicted that Thor the Thunder God will kill the enormous snake but fall victim to the poison of the serpent.

Thor as per the volva, is expected to walk for nine inches before falling. When he dies the sky will become dark and the entire world will be engulfed by flames. The earth will then be covered in water until it rises once with more fertility than it was before. Magni and Modi took over Mjolnir after the death of their father.

The TYR

Tyr is considered to be to be a minor god within Norse mythology, but prior to the Age of the Vikings they were considered the most powerful god of all. Tyr is also identified as Teiws Tiw, T'waz, Cyo, Tius, Tio and Ziu.

Tyr is in the end, the successor to Dyeus The archetypal father god from The Proto-Indo-

European period. Tyr was godfather prior to the time that Odin was introduced into the scene. Different versions of his tale claim the following: Tyr could be the father of Odin.

Tyr was the first Norse God of War. In the time that Vikings were in control in the Migration Age and Tyr's popularity fell and he was replaced with Odin or Thor. The belief is that Vikings were not averse to the traits of Tyr who were more about bravery and strength on the field.

In combat, the Norsemen were adamant about the power of their strength as well as wisdom and strategy that was more like Odin or Thor. However, Tyr is still a significant figure within Norse mythology. In fact, he's one of the few gods that were immortalized with the day named after the gods. Tuesday is named after Dyeus' Day or Tiw's Day.

Tyr is the epitome masculinity. He is renowned for his strength and courage and for his heroic actions during combat. Indeed, some sources refer to him as"the "boldest among the Norse Gods". Tyr is also as a hero of splendor, honor as well as law and justice.

Men would create Tyr's symbol that is the T-Rune (resembles an arrow pointed upwards) on their weapons to give them to God in exchange for victory in battle. The legend of Norse heroic hero Sigurd was once instructed by Valkyrie Sigrdrifa to invoke Tyr to win combat.

Tyr is often depicted as having long hair and a hand. In that hand, he carried a spear that was used during combat. The reason for Tyr's dismembered hand is based on Fenrir One among the kids of Loki.

Through prophecies, gods believed the Wolf Fenrir was going to cause a lot of troubles for them. Odin brought Fenrir along with his brothers brought to his. Odin toss Hel in Niflheim and Jormungand into the deep sea.

He left Fenrir in the hands of gods. Tyr is the sole one brave enough to feed the Wolf. This is the reason Tyr is often referred to by the name of"the "feeder of the Wolf". As Fenrir increased in size in a very short time, the gods were worried. They conspired to bound Fenrir to shield their own from being a victim of the curse. So the gods attempted to tie a rope around his neck, but the wolf refused to let the tie.

To show trustworthiness, Fenrir asked one of gods to put his or her hand in his mouth. If anyone did this it would be clear that gods didn't intend to do any harm for him. Tyr due to his bravery, offered to help and put his hands inside the mouth of the wolf.

After the gods successfully wrapped the cord around the neck of Fenrir, the wolf attempted to break free , but was unsuccessful. Naturally, Fenrir cut off his right arm of Tyr and cut it off around the wrist. Due to this, the wrist is also beginning to be called"the "wolf-joint".

Tyr also passed away during Ragnarok. He was able to kill Garm another of the guardians from hell before succumbing the the injuries caused by the hound.

LOKI

It is the Norse Trickster God known also as Loke, Loder, Lokkju, Lopter, Lopti, Loki-Laufeyjarson. The most appropriate description of this "adopted" god of Odin and the brother of Thor is that he's an rascal.

Loki the Lad had his fair share of mischievous and malicious adventures that certainly brought him the attention of not just a few gods human beings, as well as other species. The grandparents of Loki were giants Laufey and Faurbati. Odin took his father's life but in lieu of killing his newborn giant, he chose to keep him alive and treat Loki as his own son , though some claim that he never adopted Loki.

One of the most hilarious stories about Loki was that some of his tricks resulted in his balls being attached to the back of a goat. This occurred after Loki, the God of Mischief caused the death of Skaldi's giantess father. She took on Asgard and demanded they make her laugh , so she could stop and leave. Loki was successful by making Asgard laugh by using his trick of pulling the ball.

Loki was the one behind the clever plan to hire the services of a giant for the wall that the Norse gods had built to defend Asgard. But, the giant was looking for to have the Sun in addition to the Moon in exchange in exchange for the services he rendered. Also, he wanted to possess Freya who he can get when he completes his wall in the amount of time that was agreed on. It was expected that the gods and goddesses weren't favorable to the arrangement. Loki however, convinced everyone that everything will be well since he's sure that the giant won't finish the task on time.

It's interesting that what Loki and the gods of other gods hadn't anticipated to be surprised was the fact that the gigantic was able to have the stallion Svadilfari. He was able accomplish his mission without difficulty due to the stallion that helped in hauling the boulders to construct the wall. With just three days left the wall was almost completed and everyone, particularly Freya was becoming anxious.

Loki utilized his ability to change shape to transform into a mare and entice Svadilfari out of his task. Loki did a great job of dragging Svadilfari into the woods , thus preventing the giant from completing his obligation.

The cheeky Loki was also involved in the development of Mjolnir his brother Thor's Hammer. Loki made a bet Brokkr, the dwarf. Brokkr on the basis that their brother legendary craftsman Sindri (also also known as Eitri) could not create anything superior to the ones that they Sons of Ivaldi have made.

The Sons of Ivaldi was a group of dwarves who constructed Freyr's ship Freyr and also designed Odin's spear as well as the Skidbladnir and the Gungir. Sindri, who was up for the challenge, set to work on a few things. Of of course, Loki will not let himself be defeated by two dwarfs. As Brokkr was working on the bellows Loki transformed into a fly, and attacked the dwarf with the arm.

He was expecting Brokkr to feel the discomfort and stop pumping the bellows, thereby impacting their work. But Brokkr was stubborn and continued to pump. When Sindri was back to pull out the skins of pigs which he had previously put inside the forge ended up with Gullinbursti the boar from Freyr.

Sindri then placed some gold in the forge, and instructed his brother to continue in the bellows' hum until he returned. Loki returned and smacked Brokkr in the neck two times but the dwarf would not budge. What was the result was Draupnir the Draupnir, the ring of Odin. Sindri then put the iron piece into the forge and requested Brokkr to crank the bellows a second time.

Loki who was disguised as a fly returned and smacked the eyelid of the dwarf which caused a bleed and forced Brokkr to sit down and wash his eyes. In the midst of this gap, the hammer that was created had a smaller handle than the one originally planned, and was held with only one hand. This hammer would be Thor's most powerful weapon, Mjolnir.

The creations of the brother were so impressively designed that the gods lent their vote to the brothers. Thus, the dwarves won their bet against Loki in the midst of preparing to cut off his head, but Loki's god pushed him out of the situation by announcing that his neck (which required to be cut to gain access to his head) was not part of the bargain.

BALDR

A son to Odin as well as Frigg, Baldr was one of the most sought-after Asgardian gods. Baldr was known as the God of Beauty, Light and Joy. Baldr is also known in the form of Balder and Baldur had a marriage to Nanna who was his mother. He was blessed with Nep as well as Forseti. Baldr was a resident of Breidablik.

Baldr has always fantasized about dying. His mother, inquiring about his visions, demanded all and anything to not cause harm to her son. However, Loki, who was angry Loki did not want any of this.

In disguise, he played Frigg to reveal Baldr's sole weakness: mistletoe. Frigg in her search to force every living thing and object take the pledge to never hurt Baldr she deemed that it was unnecessary to demand to do the same for the little mistletoe.

Loki looked for the mistletoe, and then had Hod (the Blind Hod (Hodr) to throw it towards his younger brother like darts in one of their games of fun. Due to Frigg's mistake, the mistletoe hit Bladr's spleen and he perished. However, Loki was not done however. After Odin made Hermod in Hel for a plead for Baldr the goddess of Death was in agreement, provided that everything be mourned in the memory of the fallen god.

All of Midgard was mourning, except for a witch called Thokk which was really Loki disguised. Due to this, Baldr was forced to live within the Underworld. Baldr's wife Nanna was also a victim of the disease following the break of her heart when her husband passed away. They were laid to rest upon a memorial pyre the ship of Baldr's Ringhorn as well as their enormous treasures as well as his horse.

The ship was then set on fire while it floated across the ocean. Loki received a sentence of death and Hod had to death by Vali. Baldr's death set off Ragnarok.

Sif

It was the Norse Corn or Maize Goddess and the wife to Thor, Sif was the Goddess of Harvest.

Sif is played in the film by Jaimie Alexander from the Thor movie series. In contrast to the black-haired protagonist in the film Sif was the Goddess of Thor. Sif had hair of gold. The reason for her hair's golden color is that it was the source of a dispute that was brewing among two brothers Thor Loki and Thor. Loki.

The sly Loki entered Sif's bedroom to cut her gorgeous hair. This caused Sif was extremely upset and caused the earth to become barren and her crops to fail to increase. Naturally her husband was angry and slapped Loki until he resisted fixing things. Loki persuaded that the brothers who dwarfed her, known as the Sons of Ivaldi, to create a new set of gold hair to be used by Sif.

Bragi

Bragi was known as the God of Eloquence. of Music and Poetry. Bragi, child of Odin and Frigg was also patron to the poets. Bragi was wed to Idunn who was the sister of Ivald and goddess of Youth and Apples.

It is typically depicted as an old man with a long white beard , holding the golden harp, and the runes of his tongue. He welcomes wounded warriors to Valhalla by playing his music.

One myth claims that Bragi was an actual person with the name Bragi Boddason. He was born in the 9th century.

There was a belief that the man was so well-known and popular poet or skald of his time. His colleagues skalds incorporated him into Norse mythology and even made him god.

Idunn

Idunn Idunn, also known as Idun, Idunn, and Ithun Idunn, also known as Idunn, Idunn and I that was believed to be the source of eternal youth. She was also recognized as the one who kept apples , as well as other fruit that ward off the aging process. Her most famous role is in Norse mythology for being the goddess who was kidnapped and taken by the gigantic Thjazi. The story began in the time Odin, Loki and Hoenir left Asgard.

They came across an ox herd and killed one to eat since they were starving. It was amazing that the meat was unable to cook after being cooked for a long time on the stove. Thjazi disguised in the form of an eagle came out and claimed he wanted to stop the meat from cooking and would only let go of his curse when the gods permit him to eat their feast.

They resisted and the eagle got the most delicious part of the oxen's meat. The angry Loki struck him with his branch , but the eagle was able to catch it and flew high, with the mischievous god in the middle. In order for the eagle to let it go Loki must swear that he would deliver Idunn and her apple to the god of giants.

When they returned after their return to Asgard, Loki told Idunn of a region brimming of fruits he encountered on the way. Idunn along and her apple, traveled with Loki to this location. She was led into the woods , where Thjazi is waiting. The giant led the woman into Thrymhein where he stayed. The gods immediately noticed the signs of aging. The gods with grey hair and wrinkles and goddesses came together and concluded that Loki was the one responsible for Idunn's disappearance.

Loki disclosed the truth and was ordered to rescue her or else he'll be executed. Loki returned as a hawk, using Freya's feathers that transform into shapes. He came across Idunn on her own in the giant's house and made her an nut to quickly grab her and fly away.

Thjazi was at home when he saw that Idunn has gone missing. He transformed into an eagle, and flew after the two. While Loki and Idunn were near Asgard and the other gods were nearby, they constructed a wall of the embers.

When the gods were secure they put the wall on fire that engulfed Thjazi and led to his death.

Ve and Vili

Ve Vili and Vili were brothers of Odin who played a significant role in the creation of the universe. They were the sons of Bestla and Bor. They were the three responsible for taking down the giant Ymir and gaining control over the universe.

After removing Ymir and end the rule of the gigantics, three of them created the first human beings - Ask or Embla. Odin provided them with soul and life. Ve gave them countenance and the ability to hear, see and speak, while Vili provided them with an intelligence and a sense of touching.

Loki said the fact that Ve and Vili were involved in an affair Frigg Odin's wife. It was during Odin's lengthy absence (exiled for his practice of "unmanly" magicians) in which all the gods believed he was dead.

Vidar

It is also known as the Wide-Ruling One, Vidar is also often referred to as Vidarr, Vithar, and Vitharr. The God of Silence and Vengeance was created by Odin through Grior. He was prophesied to be the one who would take revenge on the demise of Odin during the battle of Ragnarok by cutting Fenrir in the center of his heart.

There are other accounts that say Vidar has killed the animal by standing on its jaw and then pulling back the jaw's upper one, tearing it in pieces. This is the reason Vidar is famous for his hefty shoe, composed of pieces of leather of the shoes used by Midgardians in the past.

Vidar's revenge took place when the waters grew larger and the fire that raged from Surtr receded and let"the "Silent God" to proceed with his task.

Hod

Hod, Hodr, Hoder and Hodur. As with the other gods, the god of blindness was identified by various variants in his names. He was the son of Odin as well as Frigg and a twin brother to the well-loved Baldr. He was known as the God to Winter along with Darkness.

Baldr was murdered by Hod following Loki fooled Hod to kill him. To punish him, Hod was killed by Vali who was the daughter from Odin as well as Rindr who was born with solely the purpose of revenge against Baldr.

Forseti

Forseti is the child of Baldr and Nanna. He was known as the God in the realm of Justice and Reconciliation. He was referred to as "the the one who presided" for having court battles in his court and clearing the way to reconciliation between individuals who were at odds or factions.

Forseti is a resident of Glitnir which is comprised of a silver roof backed by gold pillars, which let the impression of a bright light that could be seen from afar. Forseti was very closely associated with meditation.

Aegir and Ran

Aegir was the God from the Ocean and is the god of all creatures living in the ocean. The couple is Ran Goddess who is the goddess of the Sea and mother of the nine billow maidens that are considered to be the spirits of the sea.

Both are members of the Jotunn race, or giants, who have long been in conflict against their Aesir gods. They however, are close to the Asgardian gods. The giants frequently invite them to their banquets. In contrast, Aegir was well-known as an affable hosting host Ran had a different reputation.

She was most responsible for the capsizing of ships, drowning sailors and living in their submerged kingdom.

Hel

Another gigantic goddess, Hel is the Goddess of Death as well as the Underworld. Her realm was called Helheim or Hel where those who died from sickness and old age remained.

She was born of an union between Loki with The giantess Angrboda. The Wolf Fenrir along with the serpent Jormungand are her twins according to the mythology of Snorri which many believe is in error.

In actual truth, some scholars consider Hel as a work of literature of poets and scholars before them. As their father Loki Three siblings were predicted to bring tragedy and trouble.

Chapter 19: Vanir Gods And Goddesses

Njord

Njord is a member from the Vanir as well as the Aesir the gods' tribes. He actually comes originally from Vanir but was taken into the Aesirs as hostage (along with his children) during the conflict among the tribal clans. Njord was known as the God for the Wind and the Sea.

He was often consulted by seafarers to ensure the safety of their voyage. It is believed that the Vanir god is associated with fertility as well as prosperity.

He was the father of Freyr and Freya through Nerthus (in certain accounts). The couple was married for only a brief period with his giantess Skadi. The giantess prayed to gods in order to get revenge for the murder of her husband Thzaji who was murdered while Idunn was being freed from his.

The gods have agreed that she could get one of them for her husband in exchange to make up for the loss. They also set Thzaji's eyes up in the sky, transforming them into stars, while Loki connected his testicles to goats in order in order to laugh at the giganticess.

In her third repair she was asked to choose one god by simply taking a look at her legs. She was tempted by Baldr but chose erroneously Njord. The marriage was not long-lasting duc to the fact that Njord preferred to reside in Noatun that was close to the sea , while Skadi preferred to live in the mountains that were covered with snow.

Freyr

Freyr, the God who was the god of Sun and rain, Freyr was also associated with abundant yields, sacral power and the virtue of virility. Also known as Frey and Yngvi The Vanir gods were also embraced from his fellow Aesirs during the Great War.

Njord is often portrayed as a man who had an upright phallus. He was well-loved by all and especially by humanity and was even described as "the greatest of gods". This is due to the fact that Freyr was the one who was responsible for their harvests, fertility , and wealth , and also facilitated peace among the. Freyr is frequently associated with Gullinborsti, the boar Gullinborsti who drives his horse. Freyr also rides on his boat Skidbladnir which shrinks to fit in his pocket.

Freyr was in love with her and later got married Gerdr who was an enormous woman. The union between her and Giant cost him his mystical sword, which could kill many by itself. Njord was forced to give up his weapon to Skirnir the messenger and shield bearer who helped him win Gerdr. He later died in

Surtr's fire since he didn't have a sword with which to fight.

Freya

Freya was the goddess for Love and Fertility. She was adored for her beauty. Freya is also was also known by the names of Gefn, Horn, Mardoll, Syr, Valfreyja, and Vanadis was connected to birth, crop gold, beauty, and sensuality.

Freya was believed to possess an ability of controlling her desires and is the most well-known seer, or volva, was shamanic. Loki was once accused Freya of having relationships with the gods as well as the elves, which could be true because of Freya's habit of seeking pleasure.

Freyja was also named an honorary members from the Aesir tribe, along with her brother and father. Freya was frequently confused with Frigga who was exactly like her. The couple she was with was Odr (who was the same as Odin) and with whom she had two daughters Hnoss as well as Gersemi.

The goddess is the keeper of Folkvangr, where half the combatants who die go. She is within the hall of her Sessrumnir.

Ull

Ull was known as the God in the realm of Justice. He was also regarded for being a god of many talents since archery was his favorite sport ski, dueling, and archery in addition to being a great hunter. Ull was also known as Oller, Uller, Ullr, Valder and Vuldr, was the son of Sif and his father was widely believed to be Egill Orvandill.

Egill was an archer of repute who Ull evidently modeled himself after. Ull is a resident of Ydalir. Although many believe Ull to belong to his Aesir tribe, others believe that he came from the Vanirs.

Ull has been described as an attractive creature who possessed the qualities of a formidable warrior. There is a belief the belief that Ull was a master of magic who utilized a magical bone specifically to cross the ocean.

Ull was the one who took over Odin as Odin, the Odin, the Lord of Asgard was banished for 10 years. He also was involved with the Elfs of Volundarkvida according to some sources.

Heimfall

A.K.A. Heimdall is the God for Light and Security Heimdall is well-known for his foresight abilities. He also has a keen ability to see and hear. Indeed, the man is able to see up to 100 miles, regardless of regardless of the light or dark.

Gullintani, as well as Gullintani the name that comes of his gold teeth. He was the daughter of nine mothers born in the middle of the earth. Helmdall has an area in Himinbjorg in which he witnessed the beginning of Ragnarok.

Heimdall is charged with protecting the bifrost from intrusion especially the giants. He is the owner of the Gjallarhorn and is the rider of Gulltopp the horse that has golden mane. He was the father of all races of humanity including peasants, serfs, and warriors -- and being the god Rig. Heimdall passed away during Ragnarok however not prior to killing Loki.

Chapter 20: Creation Of The Cosmos

The old Nordics offer a different interpretation of the story of creation. Like all stories of creation, in the beginning, there was nothing. There was just this huge expanse of empty space.

The first place to be created was the realm of fire elemental or Muspelheim or Muspell. The world was one that was ablaze with light and heat. The fire there was so intense that nobody could live there, except for those who lived there since the very beginning.

This planet was home to hot rivers that erupted into deadly waters. transformed into a solid mass. The protector for Muspelheim was a giant of fire known as Surt. Surt refers to Old Norse for "black" which could refer to the giant's charred appearance.

He sat down at the border, armed with a the flame-throwing sword. Surt took on the giants to defeat each of the Aesir as well as the Vanir gods. Surt was the one who killed Freyr and was responsible for the giant's death in the Ragnarok.

A different world was in existence and it was the world of the elemental Ice, Niflheim. This cold and icy world was completely different from Muspelheim. It was full of rain, wind and ice. A fountain named Hvergelmir is located in the middle of the Dark Land. From this fountain flowed glacial water that created the 12 rivers that run through the vacuum.

Between these two worlds was a void, referred to as the Ginnungagap which literally translates to "abyss" which translates to "yawning empty space". The ancient void was bordered by Muspelheim to the south and Niflheim to the north.

In this vacuum, the warmth of Muspell was able to interact with the coldness of Niflheim. The large volume of glacial rivers, rain and masses of ice of Niflheim together with the smoke, sparks and glowing mass of Muspellheim and caused the melting of the ice.

The melting ice made Ymir (Aurgelmir according to some reports). It was his first among the giants of frost.

The androgynous Ymir was able to reproduce sexually. He did this during the time of the creation.

After falling asleep in the hot Muspelheim, Ymir started to sweat. In the sweat of his body and sweat, more giants were born. His left arm conceived the twins of a daughter and son while his legs gave him with a son.

The frost further melted to form Audhumbla the cow that had vital milk. Ymir was able to survive by sucking nourishment-giving liquid from Audhumbla. The cow, on the other hand was licking the blocks of ice nearby to stay hydrated.

After a long day of licking, came out hairs that were dripping from salty ice. Audhumbla kept licking the frozen ice, and after two days, a complete head was visible. A few days later, Audhumbla released the whole of a beautiful and strong man. The man was Norse God, Buri.

Buri is the first Aesir gods. He had a son named Bor who was later married to Bestla, sister of Bolthorn who is also known as Boelthor. Another source says it was Ymir is the father of Bestla.

Also, she had another brother, who was not named but scholars believe him be Mimir who was later executed by the son of one Bestla's children. Bor and Bestla's marriage would be the first to be between a giant and god. Their union brought them Odin, Vili and Ve.

The three half-god, half-giant brothers would play a key role to the development of our universe. They conspired to kill Ymir and the other giants. They began with their own maternal grandfather.

After the death of Ymir Blood poured out of his body. The amount of blood flowed was so massive that the entire void was filled with it.

The remaining giants, except for Beregelmir as well as his spouse were buried in the blood of Ymir. The remaining giants were able to escape drowning by getting on a tiny boat. They later started the race of giants again.

Odin as well as his brother lifted the dead corpse of Ymir from the gushing blood. They made use of it to construct the earth that they put on top of Muspelheim in Niflheim. The flesh of the giant became earth while his blood became the ocean.

The mountains were fashioned out of his bones and the trees were created from his hair. The skull of Ymir was also transformed and four bones-shaped pillars into the sky or the Vault of Heaven. The gods created one dwarf to protect every corner of the sky.

The names are North, South, East and West. The brains of Ymir's were thrown into the sky and transformed into clouds. In the Vault of Heavens it was believed that the gods protected the sparks and burning embers of flame from Muspelheim and later, the sun, moon , and stars.

They controlled the movements of the celestial bodies that resulted in the creation of day and night, in addition to the summer and winter seasons. The sun's presence with its golden sunrays of light in the sky led to the development of grass.

The gods of the other gods showed up and discovered the brother's misdeeds. They aided when they created Asgard in the midst of Earth or Midgard. The story is called "The House of the Esir gods" Each of them constructed their own mansions or hall.

They also created the Bifrost as a bridge with a rainbow that gods would use to travel between Asgard up to Midgard. The god Heimdall was guarded by the Bifrost. They also utilized the giant's brows that fell to build a fence to guard their people and also the misgardians against giants.

The gods observed maggots in the decaying body of the fallen giant. They transformed them into dwarfs. The creators of the dwarves decided that they must be kept from the sun and in the earth or within the skin of Ymir.

Dwarves that are influenced by sunlight's rays became stones. They did not have children because they were all males and thus the gods chose to create two dwarf princes capable of creating other dwarfs by combining stones and soil.

Human beings of the beginning, or Midgardians were created out of tree trunks. Odin Hoenir, Odin, and Lodur were walking along the shores of the sea when they saw two trees that had damaged trunks.

Odin transformed the trees into the form of a male as well as a woman. He breathed life into the trees. Hoenir then gave souls to beings. He also granted them the power to think. The god of the other Lodur, who was their god, greeted to them warmth as well as shades of life.

In another interpretation in another version, it could be Ve as well as Vili who were with Odin on the walk. Vili provided humans with the ability to move, and the ability of understanding while Ve provided them with outfits to dress in. Vili also gave the creatures their names. Ask became the first human and Embla was the first woman. Both were the first to begin the human race.

The Nine Worlds

Upper Level

Asgard

Asgard was the name given to the land in which the Aesir gods dwelled. Odin as well as his siblings made Asgard only to serve as their home. Odin and Frigga were the rulers of this fertile heaven for the Gods.

The gods were able to fulfill their duties and responsibilities , such as deciding the fates of all the beings in the Well of Urd.

Asgard was also the place where Valhalla was situated. Valhalla is Heaven according to Norse mythology. It was believed that only those who perished during battle could be admitted to Valhalla and that Valkyries were those who carried the spirit of warriors to their final destination.

The people of Valhalla took part in a never-ending "battle". The battles were fought in the morning and, at night, they rehabilitated and their injured limbs were rehabilitated.

In the evening the warriors shared stories about the battle of the day and ate a big meal drinking, dancing, and drinking heavily. Bifrost: Bifrost links Asgard to the heavens.

Vanaheim

The Vanir gods lived in Vanaheim. The Vanaheim realm was believed to be located to the west of Asgard because Njord was a migratory god who traveled to the east from Vanaheim toward Asgard.

Alfheim

Alfheim was home to The Light Elves which were godlike creatures. Freyr was a member of The Vanir clan was head of the kingdom of the elves, which made many scholars bewildered.

There was no direct connection to these two gods Vanir gods or the Elves,, which resulted in this bit of information being very difficult to understand.

Middle Level

Midgard

Odin was the main reason for the birth of Midgard which is the place where humans reside. Odin and his brothers defeated the gigantic Ymir and then from his dead body, poured blood that brought about the demise of all frost giants , save for one , Bergelmir.

The corpse of the dead giant was transformed to Midgard through Odin. The flesh of Ymir became the earth, his blood turned into sea and his skull transformed into the skies. His bones turned into mountains and trees were formed by his hair.

Odin also employed the giant's eyebrow to create a barrier between the human race. From Ymir's corpse, the World Tree Yggdrasil grew and protected the world by its branches. It was located in Midgard the place where Odn as well as the gods erected the first human beings - Ask And Embla.

Jotunheim

Another character from the Nordic tales was the giants, or Jotnars. These giants lived in Jotunheim. The inhabitants of Jotunheim were not popular with many. They not only terrorized misgardians, but also the gods too.

King Thyrm was the ruler of Jotunheim, the land of the giants, which was divided from the world by the River Ifing From Asgard.

Jotunheim was the capital city of Jotunheim is Utgard which was the main fortress which surrounded the kingdom.

Svartalfheim

There are Svartalfars also known as Dark Elves call Svartalfheim their home. They are Dark Elves are the same as the dwarves prominent in many Norse stories.

The most popular dwarfs are known as those of the Sons of Ivaldi. The people of the realm are featured in the film Thor: The Dark World as the principal antagonists.

Lower Level

Nidavellir

The dwarves Gods made from maggots are beneath the earth. They live in caves and mountains. Nidavellir The Home of the Dwarves, was under the rule of Hreidmar. The dwarves are famous for their craft. They were the ones responsible for the creation of Mjolnir and Gungir as well as other.

Muspelheim

In the realm of fire Muspelheim and is controlled by Surtr. Surtr. He may be associated with Sinmara. In the real world, dwell Eldjotnars, the fire giants.

Sometimes, they were known as the Sons Muspell as well as the Muspellssynirs. The were among the people capable of destroying the Bifrost.

Niflheim

Niflheim is, as we have said, is the reverse to the realm of Muspelheim. While Muspelheim is a world that is fueled by fire, the first is made up of Ice. Niflheim is also known as the Mist World due to the fact that it is surrounded by mist and is surrounded by darkness. Following It was created by the universe Gods changed Niflheim into the home of dead. It is also called Helheim. The lowest of all the realms Helheim will be where dead go after their time on earth has come ended.

Niflheim is controlled by Hel and guarded by dog Garm.

Chapter 21: What We Can Utilize Viking Information Today

The Vikings were the conquerors. They had an incredible capacity to build wooden ships capable of enduring long voyages and treacherous oceans, that they left this world with a wealth of ideas.

A major and significant characteristics to the Vikings was their ability to create trade relations that benefitted their society the greatest. The explorers and traders traveled all over the world to bring back goods from foreign countries.

If you study how the Norse individuals and the Viking travels, it is easy to realize that a lot trading routes, the income that was generated for Europe and the resources of Europe originate from these relationships that were long-standing. Nowadays, Scandinavia would be suffering from lower economies if they do not have long-lasting relations with a variety of nations.

It is possible to transition from plundering and pillaging to trade relations that yield important resources. The world is in crisis today.

North Korea is a good example of a country that is willing to do everything it can regardless of the means and at the same time, other nations attempt to safeguard their scarce resources. The Vikings were able to establish the situation of sharing the little they could from their cold and icy landscape to acquire what they required.

The Viking culture was responsible for changing the economics of Europe from the beginning of AD periods into an economic system dominated by merchants. There was no concern with high-end trade in goods and more about providing people what they needed to live.

Vikings established markets, which provided employment that was accessible as well as helping to establish currency in Europe as a way of trading and advancing the civilization.

Looking back at Democracy

The Vikings are among the first societies to create the system of democratic government that has lasted for many decades. It's true that Rome as well as Greece had their own systems however it was the Viking society that helped create the world as we see it today. It was the Viking Althing was the first national assembly in Europe which brought the idea of modern day parliament across the borders of several nations. Women were not allowed to vote, their belief system considered women as the same as men. Take a look at Freyja and the other goddesses from Norse Mythology, as a method of proving women as warriors. Women were able to manage their homes as well as their farms and even own their own their own land. There are places across the planet where women aren't permitted to enjoy the same freedom as Vikings women had. Their democratic and social practices could teach other societies that maybe it's good to see females as equal before the eye of God and humans.

There are certain things that the Vikings could be guilty of that they considered shady and for which they had Loki to take the blame. If you consider their ability to design ships that traveled long distances as well as weapons with large ranges, and the technology to improve their culture over others during a time of war, we can still take lessons from the past.

Conclusion

There's nothing as powerful as the power of mythology to inspire us to consider other people and their places. The heroic feats of legends and the grotesque actions of monsters, the vastness of epic stories--all of them transport us to another world. Myths serve an important purpose in that they help remind us of our identity and the way we ought to (and ought not) behave. They also help people understand all over the world before the development of technology and science and provide peace in times of conflict and shortages.

Norse mythology is distinct because the people who wrote these stories and the people who practiced their religions were also peoples that became known as the "Vikings"-- legendary characters as such. Therefore, Norse mythology is tied to certain themes: the significance of the warrior-hero inherent human character of all creatures, whether either supernatural or not; and the significance of territoriality and the reputation of characters that appear in the entire canon. Norse mythology also was significantly affected by the subsequent Christianization of their land as well as the demise of the Viking lifestyle; this gives a dark and sometimes glorious feel to the majority of the mythological materials. This expands the possibilities of Norse mythology, and offer some semblance of something for everyone. This is the reason for its continued popularity.

www.ingramcontent.com/pod-product-compliance
Lightning Source LLC
Chambersburg PA
CBHW050023130526
44590CB00042B/1862